Ubi Caritas

Ubi Caritas

Facing the Crisis in Consecrated Life Today

Brother René Stockman

© 2007 Novalis, Saint Paul University, Ottawa, Canada

Cover Photo: Paul Hamel

Layout: Christiane Lemire

Business Offices:

Novalis Publishing Inc.
10 Lower Spadina Avenue, Suite 400
Toronto, Ontario, Canada
M5V 2Z2

Novalis Publishing Inc.
4475 Frontenac Street
Montréal, Québec, Canada
H2H 2S2

Phone: 1-800-387-7164
Fax: 1-800-204-4140
E-mail: books@novalis.ca
www.novalis.ca

Library and Archives Canada Cataloguing in Publication

Stockman, René

Ubi caritas: facing the crisis in consecrated life today / René Stockman.

Translation of Ubi caritas: godgewijd leven, published 2000.
Includes bibliographical references.
ISBN 978-2-89507-905-7

1. Monastic and religious life. 2. Monasticism and religious orders.
I. Title.

BX2435.S745 2007   255   C2007-903851-4

Printed in Canada.

All rights reserved. No part of this publication may be reproduced, stored in a retrieval system, or transmitted in any form, or by any means, electronic, mechanical, photocopying, recording, or otherwise, without the written permission of the publisher.

The Scripture quotations contained herein are from the New Revised Standard Version of the Bible, copyrighted 1989 by the Division of Christian Education of the National Council of the Churches of Christ in the United States of America, and are used by permission. All rights reserved.

We acknowledge the financial support of the Government of Canada through the Book Publishing Industry Development Program (BPIDP) for our publishing activities.

5 4 3 2 1   11 10 09 08 07

Contents

Preface 7

1. A Spirituality 9
2. A Way of Life 16
3. A New Challenge 25
4. Our Vows 37
5. Making Room in Our Hearts 51
6. United in God 62
7. Religious Leadership 76
8. Moved by Charity 98
9. Growing Older 122
10. Vocations 137
11. The Future 151

Notes 163

Preface

In 1996, the publication of *Vita Consecrata* breathed some fresh air into consecrated life. The biblical story of the disciples' experience with Jesus at his transfiguration became a new symbol for consecrated life, reflecting the mystery of both vocation and election. This breath of fresh air started things stirring: from the local to the international level, people got together to study the document and to discuss the future of religious life. They returned home renewed, claiming they had seen the Lord (Mark 9:2-8).

Theologians began to show fresh interest in consecrated life, and several books were published on the topic. *The Fire in These Ashes* by Joan Chittister reflects the tone of the writing of those years. As religious struggled to clarify their identity and to define their place within the church and society, terms such as "prophetic" and "liminal" were used to describe consecrated life.

My own experience of those years, along with my research on the church, prompted me to write this book on the future of consecrated life. It draws on both the experiences of other religious and their feedback to my talks on the subject. Though originally written for members of my own community, all consecrated people may find it a helpful roadmap as we seek to clarify our identity within the church and society.

Like the disciples after the transfiguration, may our encounter with the Lord bring renewed energy and new life!

Brother René Stockman
Brother of Charity

1

A Spirituality

My father was a blacksmith. On holidays he would ask me to help him for a short while before he'd send me out to play again. He knew there was little use investing in the future if no one was trained to take over the smithy. As farmers started using machines instead of workhorses, my father was confronted with a new situation. There was no place for his skills in the world of tractors; his equipment and tools now stand in a museum for industrial technology. He never visited the museum. "That page has been turned," he would say.

Timothy Radcliffe, the former master of the Dominicans, describes members of religious congregations as blacksmiths living in the era of cars. Religious men and women are looking for a new purpose for their lives, fearing that they, too, will someday end up in a museum. While museums are important, not everyone and everything belongs in one.

Today's shopping malls and bars are full of life, but religious are still drawn to places where people are suffering or lonely. In the future, will religious be found in museums or in malls? Will we live in convents or among the poor? Rather than an either/or situation, it needs to be a both/and situation. Religious are, and will continue to be, involved in a variety of settings. Religious life has never been limited to one specific location or lifestyle. Religious remain ever changing in a world that is ever changing. Only our core remains unchanged.

In her book *The Fire in These Ashes: A Spirituality of Contemporary Religious Life*, Joan Chittister writes, "The spirituality of our times is a spirituality of Easter Saturday: a spirituality of confusion and bewilderment, of incompetence and incapacity, of faith in the darkness and of the power of hope. It is a spirituality that lives on, even when that seems useless."[1] This definition is a good description of the experience of consecrated life today. Religious who live with a spirituality of Easter Saturday believe that Easter is coming, but know that signs of new life and resurrection are hard to find. Or do we fail to see these signs?

Beyond the statistics

Recently, newspapers reported that for the last few years, the number of religious in Belgium has fallen by 550 each year. An oft-repeated joke asks, "Where does one find most sisters and brothers these days?" The answer: "In the obituaries in newspapers."

In 2002, there were 10,924 sisters in Flanders; three years later, there were 9,521. In 2002, there were 3,039 male religious; three years later, there were 2,754.[2] Similar figures are found throughout Western Europe: there are few religious vocations, many deaths, and an increase in the average age of those who remain.

From a worldwide perspective, Europe shows the greatest decline in numbers. In 2002, the number of male religious decreased by 874, and the number of female religious by 9,755. In the same year, Europe still had the highest number of religious: 430,000 of the global total of 971,000. Asia and Africa are the only areas where there was a slight increase. In the United States the numbers are decreasing steadily; every year there are 4,000 fewer sisters and 500 fewer male religious.

These global statistics do not paint a positive picture of religious life. Overall, there has been an annual decline of 10,000. If we focus on these statistics alone, there is little reason to be optimistic. However, we can still remain hopeful despite these numbers. *Optimism* is directly linked with our efforts; being *hopeful* has to do with trusting God. We can learn from these statistics without allowing them to determine our future.

Because the average age of religious is increasing, a smaller group within each order and congregation is now responsible for looking after the elderly members. As more and more energy is needed to care for these elderly members, many in leadership positions are becoming discouraged. These leaders are also concerned about the legacy of their community, and their own survival. As a result, many congregations lack the resources or motivation to focus on the work they were founded to do. Others continue their work as best they can but eventually must let go. Many brothers and sisters ask themselves, "Have our lives been useless and meaningless?"

There is little energy for new internal or external initiatives. In the past, religious used to be active wherever people needed help. Today, they are being replaced by lay people who are responding from humanitarian motives, and not out of religious conviction.

Many religious have one overriding concern these days: to survive until the last person has left religious life or has died. They tend to live in the past and not in the present.

This description of the situation may sound extreme, which it is, to a certain extent. But some religious are responding to the decrease in numbers and the aging of their members with hope, concerned about more than simply preserving their legacy and ensuring their survival. These religious are realistic; they do not hide from the facts. They look for ways to continue to shape consecrated life given the changing circumstances and times. They continue to believe that their vocation is lifelong, as is their mission. When asked about the number of religious vocations in his province, one provincial superior answered, "200!" Noting the surprise on their faces at this high number, he was more specific. "There are 200 brothers in my province," he said. "I hope that all of them still live with a sense of vocation."

At the end of the 1970s, theologian J. B. Metz coined the term *ars moriendi,* or the art of dying, as a positive dimension of all life on earth.[3] This term was his response to the possible demise of religious life. Nothing on earth lasts forever: everything is born, grows, blossoms, dies and eventually disappears. Why should this not be true for religious orders or congregations?

Timothy Radcliffe once said in a meeting, "The Holy Spirit was able to manage without the Dominicans for twelve centuries. Maybe a time will come when the Spirit will be able to manage without the Dominicans again."[4]

Some religious draw strength and courage from the biblical understanding that times of abandonment and exile were usually times of purification from which people emerged with renewed resources. Times of trial can be opportunities by which we deepen or revive our relationships with God. Several Old Testament texts show that we are more likely to turn to God during a crisis than when everything is going well. Despite his misery, Job could say, "For I know that my Redeemer lives, and that at the last he will stand upon the earth; and after my skin has been thus destroyed, then in my flesh shall I see God, whom I shall see on my side, and my eyes shall behold, and not another. My heart faints within me" (Job 19:25-27). In the book of Habakkuk, we read, "Though the fig tree does not blossom, and no fruit is on the vines, though the produce of the olive fails and the fields yield no food; though the flock is cut off from the fold and there is no herd in the stalls, yet I will rejoice in the Lord; I will exult in the God of my salvation" (Habakkuk 3:17-18). Theologian Cornelius Ernst used to say, "Grace is given whenever we rejoice in the Lord in spite of our despair."[5]

Certainly some orders and congregations will disappear. These groups will need to embrace the concept of *ars moriendi* in order to develop a spirituality of gratitude for what has been. It is to be hoped that they will not become defeatist and disappointed, dwelling only on the past. Religious must understand that, both as a group and as individuals, we are called to remain true to our vocation until the very last day.

Other orders and congregations will continue to exist. That fact might make others question why they are not able to survive, what they did wrong or whether it was all a waste of time. In Flanders, over the past two centuries, many local initiatives were begun to meet the emerging needs. Schools, hospitals and retirement homes often were founded by a parish priest or local clergy, who in turn created a congregation to run those institutions. Today, the apostolic role of those congregations no longer exists. Society now meets those needs, and we must be grateful for that.

This does not mean, however, that the Christian community in general, and religious congregations in particular, shouldn't be involved in the fields of education and nursing. But the initial charism, and especially its secular aspect, can no longer be the sole focus of congregations. If new congregations are to be founded these days, they will not be running schools or hospitals. They will likely focus on a variety of other material and spiritual needs. Congregations that have not adapted to the emerging needs of society will have no future in this context.

Some congregations have been able to adapt to the changes in society and are continuing to create a distinct role for themselves, finding new ways to meet needs as they emerge. Because of their ability to adapt, while remaining true to their charism, these congregations are flourishing today.

Other congregations have expanded internationally, a move that has led to a much broader perspective. They are developing new types of collaboration across the continents and have members from many nationalities.

In trying to understand why some communities survive, I think back to my father and his work as a blacksmith. Unlike my father, other blacksmiths chose to become mechanics. Those who survived were able to adapt to the changing needs in an ever-changing world.

The story continues

Beyond the orders and congregations that will survive these changing needs, some fresh growth is visible. Some affiliated groups have grown out of the original congregations' charisms. Also, some entirely new movements, some of which may eventually develop into religious communities, are emerging.

Who are these affiliated groups? Some include people who embrace the spirituality of the congregation with whom they work. Many schools and hospitals, originally founded by religious congregations, have become society's responsibility. Several of these institutions have mission statements based on the charism of the original congregation. Although few or no religious are currently active in the institution, the work is being carried on in the same spirit.

Another important group includes former students who were influenced by the congregation's values while attending school. Many people have fond memories of a certain sister or brother who taught them. Here are a few examples of personal stories people have told me.

Some time ago, I was standing at a train station with an elderly brother who had spent his life caring for psychiatric patients. A couple standing nearby recognized him and came over to talk with us. They told how my companion had nursed the husband more than thirty years before. They were extremely grateful and said that they had managed to get through that difficult period in their lives due to the help, care and encouragement of this brother.

Another time, at a conference, I saw a man standing nearby, clearly mustering his courage to speak with me. Approaching me, he said that his son, who had a serious disability, had stayed at one of our institutions. He told me how a brother had comforted him on his first visit to his son. He added, "That brother did not just work there; he actually lived with the children. He was a real father to them."

For eight years I was the head of a psychiatric hospital and principal of a school for psychiatric nurses. Our convent was located in the same building as the hospital and school. During a visit to one of the wards, a patient said, "Brother, you are one of us since you sleep here, too." That patient expressed what many felt intuitively: a sense of security due to our shared living space.

Today, many lay people want to work with an order or congregation in a deeply committed way. Members of third orders and associate members keep their lay status while developing their spirituality based on the order or congregation's charism. (I deal extensively with this new development to religious life in Chapter 11.)

Apart from the affiliated groups, new movements and communities are developing into religious communities. They deserve our attention and support because they are living proof that the Holy Spirit is working among us. These new movements are breathing fresh air into the church! It is good to be in dialogue with them, and to help create a space so they can grow. We do well to support them, and to not force them to fit our way of thinking.

It is also important that we do not compete with one another. Some religious wonder why these emerging movements seem so innovative. These new communities truly seek God in order to love and to serve God and to proclaim the Good News, and at times they do so in a lively manner. Some members of these new movements claim that they are carrying on the work that congregations used to do. This attitude tends to deny a place for traditional congregations in church and society. Instead, these new movements need to introduce a new charism and, together with the existing congregations, revive, enrich and improve the image of consecrated life in the church.

2

A Way of Life

We are all called to live in ways that are pleasing to God and others. Every life – single, married or consecrated – offers a framework within which we answer that call. Consecrated life must always be seen within our fundamental call in life. Before examining consecrated life specifically, I will consider it within the full range of lifestyle choices, being careful not to set it apart from the others (which has happened in the past).

There are many ways to describe a vocation, but I like to start from a personal question: "How can we develop our lives in a way that it is pleasing to God and to others?" Our lives exist between two poles: our actual reality and an ideal situation towards which we strive. Paul alludes to his experience of these two poles: "I do not do the good I want, but the evil I do not want is what I do" (Romans 7:19). The Brothers of Charity's Rule of Life expresses this idea also: "Like everyone else, you ask: What is the meaning of my existence? What is the significance of my life? You have doubts and seek assurance. You cannot explain everything in your life, for your life is partly shrouded in mystery. You will never find an adequate answer to the simplest questions concerning your behaviour and your activity."[6]

It is important to consider consecrated life within the mystery of human existence. Every choice we make invites us to start from reality and to move towards an ideal. This does not mean that we deny or avoid our reality. Nor should we create an imaginary world or live an imaginary life. We try to become pleasing to God and to others *within* our lives. If the choice to live a consecrated life does not help us respond to God's call, then we have missed the point. Put theologically, God wants to be part of our lives, and our human reality becomes the expression of that divine reality.

Know, accept and love yourself

"Self-knowledge is the beginning of wisdom." This old Flemish saying shows how important it is to know ourselves while acknowledging that it is a lifelong process. The search to know ourselves is limited by our tendency to deny or distort the truth about ourselves. Often we do not want to face the truth of who we really are; instead, we choose to live in a world of illusion. We have the tendency to ignore or hide from reality, and sometimes we succeed in fooling ourselves. This distorted image of ourselves can be compared to an adjustable mirror used to treat patients with anorexia nervosa. Despite being extremely thin, these patients still believe that they are larger than they really are. Similarly, the mirror in which we see ourselves can correct certain features, making us think we look better than we do.

We need courage and insight to examine the depths of our being, to face our escapist tendencies, and to reveal our true nature. At times, we can be like Zacchaeus, who climbed a tree to see Jesus. Perhaps Zacchaeus didn't like the fact that he was short and he wanted to appear taller than he actually was. Jesus invited Zacchaeus to climb down from the tree and to eat with him in his own home (Luke 19:1-10). Jesus accepted Zacchaeus as he was, calling him to be more truly himself.

After criticizing the scribes for praying only in public places, Jesus taught his followers how to pray: "Whenever you pray, go into your room and shut the door and pray to your Father who is in secret; and your Father who sees in secret will reward you" (Matthew 6:6). Jesus urged his listeners to turn within to be with God in that quiet and solitary place.

The psalmist knew how hard it is to search for self-knowledge. We need help from the One who created us, who knows our innermost being: "O Lord, you have searched me and known me. You know when I sit down and when I rise up; you discern my thoughts from far away. You search out my path and my lying down, and are acquainted with all my ways" (Psalm 139:1-3). Our efforts to know ourselves, and to become more ourselves, must be grounded in prayer where God meets us with his knowledge of our innermost being. Based on that self-knowledge, we can begin to see ourselves more accurately. The psalmist writes: "O Lord, my heart is not lifted up, my eyes are not raised too high; I do not occupy myself with things too great and too marvellous for me" (Psalm 131:1).

However, self-knowledge is only the first step that leads us to *accepting* ourselves, and then to *loving* ourselves. Having discovered who we really are, we have to accept ourselves as we are. Many people find it difficult to accept themselves as they really are. I am not referring to physical imperfections that we may try to correct or cover up through cosmetics. I am referring to the unpleasant or annoying characteristics that we try to hide from others. Some people were not affirmed as children, and as adults they continue to feel inferior, thinking they are worthless.

Ultimately, we need to accept ourselves as a mysterious mixture of good and evil. A well-known Flemish expression says, "Nothing that is human is foreign to us." Overestimating ourselves or feeling inferior to others are common traps. As we get to know ourselves we need to learn to accept ourselves and to be more truly ourselves.

Only self-acceptance can help us to love ourselves eventually. Jesus places love of self on the same level as love of our neighbours, and compares both to love of God (Matthew 22:34-40; Mark 12:28-34; Luke 10:25-28). If we believe that God created us, how can we hate ourselves? If we love only God and our neighbour, and not ourselves, we are not following Jesus' commandment to love God, found within our very being. It is precisely in loving ourselves that we become pleasing to God and to others. By knowing, accepting and loving ourselves, we live according to Jesus' teaching. But all our efforts must be grounded in love – from our own self-knowledge to our self-acceptance. Becoming pleasing to God and others includes both dealing mercifully with the evil in us, and developing the good in us.

What prevents us from being pleasing to God?

Facing our true selves brings us face to face with both the positive and negatives aspects of ourselves. Facing the negative aspects of our personality can be very painful. Often we react by ignoring them or pretending they do not exist. We want to believe there is no such thing as evil. But however hard we try to ignore evil, we have to admit that it exists. It is there, hidden deep inside each one of us. We can recognize its power and the disastrous consequences it has.

When these negative traits surface they can be upsetting, and we may want to bury what has emerged. When that happens we behave like the man who received only one talent and who buried it in a hole for fear of losing it (Matthew 25:14).

Many perfectionists struggle to accept the reality of evil within themselves. They hold very high expectations of themselves, and they are often tense because they fear that their coping strategies will fail. They place a heavy yoke on their own shoulders, thinking that they can overcome evil on their own. To some extent, they succeed but they end up living with a lot of stress. Perfectionists are often proud people who think that they can bring about justice through their own efforts. But their struggle against evil is focused on themselves, forgetting the call to become pleasing to God and others. Their main objective is to become pleasing to themselves.

Paul challenges those who put a heavy yoke on their own shoulders, saying they reject the freedom that Christ offers. "For freedom Christ has set us free. Stand firm, therefore, and do not submit again to a yoke of slavery" (Galatians 5:1). Those who try to impose all kinds of rules and regulations on themselves deprive themselves of the freedom that Jesus offers. God does not want us to be perfect according to our standards, but according to his. And that standard has nothing to do with fear or heavy burdens. Fear often leads to aggression, which becomes a struggle to suppress evil by dealing harshly with ourselves.

Life becomes one long litany of stresses that can lead to nervous exhaustion. Many neurotic disorders and psychosomatic complaints are caused by the aggressive way we deal with ourselves. Jung called this guilt complex "a disease that turns people into tormented, plagued creatures who are almost suffocated by their own feelings of guilt."[7] Asceticism, often associated with self-punishment and penance, becomes a way to make up for our sins and guilt.

But does God really want penance? Asceticism developed from the concept of a punishing God, and humans projected that image of God onto themselves by denying reality and by punishing themselves constantly. Have we forgotten that God is a merciful God? We need to let go of trying to overcome evil by ourselves, and instead rely on God's mercy.

When Jesus was criticized for sharing his food with sinners and tax collectors, he said that it is those who are sick who need a physician, and not those who are well (Matthew 9:13). Using words from Hosea, he said, "I desire mercy, not sacrifice" (Matthew 9:13; Hosea 6:6). In our struggle against evil we need to develop an attitude of mercy towards ourselves. The mercy that Jesus showed to sinners is the kind of mercy that we should demonstrate to all sinners, including ourselves.

Dealing with the evil within us means facing the wrongs we have done. It means daring to say, "This action is wrong because it is not pleasing to God. It goes against my development as a human being and prevents the love within me from deepening." By admitting that we are sorry for our wrongdoing, we ask God for forgiveness. But if we do not let go of our feelings of guilt we have not taken God's forgiveness seriously. If we hold on to our guilt, we deny God's mercy. When God forgives us – and God is always prepared to forgive us – we need to forgive ourselves, too. We must not keep tormenting ourselves with guilt or hurting ourselves by living with fear.

Jesus' message is one of liberation. But often we resist the implication of that message. We should be overwhelmed by God's great mercy; indeed, there is nothing greater than that. Paul boasted about his weaknesses because it is through those very weaknesses that God shows his mercy. "The Lord said to me, 'My grace is sufficient for you, for power is made perfect in weakness.' So, I will boast all the more gladly of my weaknesses, so that the power of Christ may dwell in me. Therefore I am content with weaknesses, insults, hardships, persecutions, and calamities for the sake of Christ; for whenever I am weak, then I am strong" (2 Corinthians 12:9-10). When we are weak we are in the ideal space to let God become fully God in our lives. Only through God's mercy and strength can we start living our lives fully.

The Carmelite Brother Laurent (1608–1691) understood Paul's words: "When I have made a mistake, I do nothing else than admit it and tell God about it: 'I am afraid that I shall never be able to act differently, if you leave me to sort things out myself. You alone can prevent my fall, and you alone can right what I have done wrong.' Having said that, I no longer worry about the wrong that I have done."[8] When God reveals his mercy, we are filled with a grace that gives us the strength both to turn away from evil *and* to turn towards all that is good.

In *Heaven Begins Within You: Wisdom from the Desert Fathers*, Anselm Grün develops the idea of "a spirituality from below."[9] He challenges us to make peace with our enemies and to use our energy to foster good. Thanks to God's mercy we can redirect the energy that is otherwise sucked in a negative direction by evil.

The way to the good

God's mercy goes beyond forgiveness by giving us the strength to keep striving for the good. We need God's mercy and grace if we wish to pursue the good. Every time that God turns to us with mercy and grace, the good in us can be released.

A person who desires to do good is a person who wants to be open to God's mercy. The Jesus Prayer helps us pray for God's mercy: "Lord Jesus Christ, Son of God, have mercy on me, a sinner." When we repeat the Jesus Prayer, it starts to take root in our hearts and in our entire being. Being open to God's mercy and grace gives us the power to live in ways that are pleasing to God and others: "to clothe yourselves with the new self, created according to the likeness of God in true righteousness and holiness" (Ephesians 4:24). We are called to live in God's image and we need God's grace to fulfill that calling.

True asceticism consists in eliminating all that keeps us from following our calling. It focuses on the positive aspects of our being. Our efforts to overcome any negative characteristics have but one purpose: to make room for the good.

Unfortunately, in striving for happiness and wanting to become fully human, we often strive after things that *fill* us – such as wealth, power and pleasure – but that do not *fulfill* us. Experience teaches us that these efforts are futile: wealth makes us crave greater wealth, power makes us thirsty for more power, pleasure makes us seek greater pleasure. We are insatiable when it comes to our passions.

Can our passions bring us happiness, or is there another way? When the gospel asks, How can we attain real life? we hear the answer: by losing it. "For all who exalt themselves will be humbled, but all who humble themselves will be exalted" (Luke 18:14). We find fulfillment when we try to become more the image and likeness of God. We find meaning and fulfillment in the fruits of the Holy Spirit: love, joy, peace, patience, kindness, generosity, faithfulness, gentleness and self-control (see Galatians 5:13-24). All that obstructs the fruits of the Holy Spirit must be cleared away so that real life can emerge.

We discover our calling in trying to follow Jesus' example of self-emptying: "who, though he was in the form of God, did not regard equality with God as something to be exploited" (Philippians 2:6). We need to identify how to best fulfill our calling. Jesus' calling was to become human, but to that purpose he accepted to give up temporarily his equality to God. In the desert the devil tempted Jesus to cling again to his divinity, which was not for that moment his calling. "He emptied himself, taking the form of a slave, being born in human likeness. And being found in human form, he humbled himself and became obedient to the point of death – even death on a cross" (Philippians 2:7-8). Like Jesus, we need to embrace, accept and love our reality since it is within our reality that we fulfill our calling.

If we want to live our lives fully we must not be driven by our passions. We need to go to the depths of our innermost selves, recognizing that we are made up of both good and bad elements. We must accept that our lives are shaped by suffering, pain, powerlessness and, eventually, death. It is this life that we must love and treat with mercy.

The key is emptying ourselves of all that fills us, but cannot fulfill us. We need to create room in our lives for the Spirit and the fruits of the Spirit. Only then can God fulfill our lives. "Therefore God also highly exalted him and gave him the name that is above every name, so that at the name of Jesus every knee should bend, in heaven and on earth and under the earth, and every tongue should confess that Jesus Christ is Lord, to the glory of God the Father" (Philippians 2:9-11).

God's mercy, seen in our weakness, can become grace and power that, in turn, enable us to live our lives to the full. Then we become pleasing to God and others.

Consecrated life is one way to live life to the full. Those who are called to consecrated life gradually discover their call, and they discover how God is the fulfillment of their lives. However, first they must pursue the path of true conversion. Consecrated life offers people the opportunity to lead a life pleasing to both God and others, but other ways of life are as meaningful and fulfilling.

The specificity of consecrated life consists in giving the first and final place to God. It is the ideal choice for those who are called to it and who seek to follow the path that is pleasing to God. However, the essential element remains the same for everyone: openness to God's mercy and grace. If consecrated life does not invite people to strive for that openness, it will eventually become a contradiction in terms. The term "consecrated life" literally means "a life devoted to God."

3

A New Challenge

Recent documents cite the importance of defining consecrated life. The definition that existed prior to Vatican II was rooted in traditions spanning several centuries. Religious life was recognizable and predictable; its appearance and structure remained unchanged for years. After Vatican II, the search for a new identity led to an initial lack of clarity. Many traditions were abandoned through this time of experimentation, and *aggiornamento* ("bringing up to date") became synonymous with a return to the original sources. Many who had felt secure within established traditions lost that frame of reference; now they were being asked to shape their lives in a more flexible way. In the past, individuality had been sacrificed for uniformity; now religious communities were becoming united in their diversity.

During the process of renewal, a lot of deconstruction and reconstruction occurred. Unfortunately, the baby was sometimes thrown out with the bathwater. Some members of religious communities, feeling that their sense of security had disappeared, abandoned ship. Others felt that religious life was not changing fast enough, but were overwhelmed by endless experiments. Sociologists were hired to study the relevance of the community's charism. Psychologists were hired to facilitate group dynamics. Convents became houses, and superiors became managers or directors. Where congregations had a more apostolic orientation, monastic practices were abandoned. In a matter of years, constitutions were rewritten and approved. A wind of change was blowing through the church and convent life.

Having functioned in isolation for centuries, congregations now looked for ways to collaborate. Novitiates were rethought at the diocesan level, leading to a reorganization of the formation of candidates, postulants, novices and young religious.

After thirty years of experimenting, the time had come to clarify the situation once again. But this did not mean a return to the past. The core of religious and consecrated life needed to be identified clearly.

Based on the council documents and post-conciliar texts, the 1995 Synod on Consecrated Life proposed a new framework. Although the synod was ambiguous and opinions were divided, the post-synodal document, *Vita Consecrata*, provided a refreshingly clear perspective. Subsequent studies about consecrated life often refer to this document. In no. 14 of *Vita Consecrata* we read, "The evangelical basis of consecrated life is to be sought in the special relationship which Jesus, in his earthly life, established with some of his disciples."[10] Joan Chittister defines consecrated life as a lifelong search for God: "A religious must be someone who seeks God and God alone, first and foremost, always and ever, and in all circumstances. He is someone who discerns the hand of God in all this confusion and uncertainty and who bears witness to God, and to God alone, whatever the situation he finds himself in."[11]

Thomas of Aquinas once said, "It is taking position at the heart of the life of God who is nothing but love: the unutterable friendship between the Father and the Son, who is the Spirit. Life, becoming alive in a way that cannot be explained, to us means finding a home in that friendship and being changed by it."[12] Any reflection on the identity of consecrated life must be situated within that search for God. It is our central core, and the charism of each congregation or order must reflect that search. Every aspect of consecrated life needs to embrace a search for God.

For a group to survive, it is important to keep that spiritual core as strong as possible, allowing it to shape the congregation's charism and our response to the challenges of our times.

Our relationship with God permits us to be in this world with all its chaos. Consecrated life loses its relevance if it becomes an escape from the world. This applies to apostolic and contemplative lives alike. Based in a loving relationship with God, we develop loving relationships with our fellow human beings. Apostolic congregations must live by their claim: inspired by the relationship with God, by prayer and spirituality, they are involved with the community, attentive to the signs of our times.

J. B. Metz states that living with a passion for God generates a passion for humanity, allowing us to see others through the eyes of God.[13] Humans are divinized when they live in God's love, and are dehumanized when they become estranged from that love. This is a challenge that consecrated people face today.

Chittister says, "What the world requires now is an example of political charity, universalism, an ecology of life, justice and peace, so that the planet should continue to exist and so that all people should be able to lead a life worthy of humankind. What religious life requires now is for religious to acquire the values and spiritual methods that should enable them to react to these new questions with personal strength, a contemplative conscience, and joint efforts."[14]

In other words, we are called to live by values that are unpopular these days but that are needed to save our world. Religious communities must always be engaged in society, bringing the gospel message to the world.

This is different from some communities' tendency to withdraw from the world and to become wrapped up with their need to survive. Such communities avoid the call to be prophetic. It is like "playing convent": a nice little get-together of like-minded people. To paraphrase a well-known expression: If religious do not serve, they serve no purpose at all.

The identity of religious life

During Vatican II and in the years following it, the vocation to religious life was analyzed and discussed. All Christians are called to become holy and to live a religious life through baptism. All the faithful are called to live from a religious perspective: focused on God and open to the spiritual dimension of life. If we restrict the term "religious" to one specific group, we risk saying that the others are non-religious. Because of this confusion, the Synod on Consecrated Life used the term "consecrated." But this term is subject to the same kind of criticism, because all the faithful are consecrated to God through their baptism. So, the term "consecrated" does not adequately reflect the specificity of religious life either.

This discussion illustrates how difficult it is to define our identity without disqualifying other people. When defining religious life in terms of a radical, exclusive and intensive call, we risk perpetuating past stereotypes of superiority. Ideally, we should be able to express the specificity of religious life without using terms that make comparisons with other lifestyles. But that is and will remain difficult despite our best efforts.

Enzo Bianchi, founder of the monastic community in Bose, Italy, tries to overcome this impasse by making "consecrated celibacy" the most specific aspect of religious life. In his book *Si tu savais le don de Dieu* (If you knew God's gift) he describes how the concept of "evangelical counsels" best defines the celibate lifestyle.[15] The gospel passage "There are [celibates] who have made themselves [celibates] for the sake of the kingdom of heaven" (Matthew 19:12) is explained in greater detail in Paul's letter to the Corinthians, where he points out that celibacy is the way to consecrate oneself undivided to God (see 1 Corinthians 7:34-35). The celibate lifestyle is a sign of God's kingdom that brings today's reality under the primacy of Christ (see 1 Corinthians 7:29, 31-32).

However, the vows taken by religious are not fully reflected by the term "evangelical counsels." These vows are grounded in gospel values that apply to all people, showing us how to live as Christians: respecting our world and all that is in it, living chastely whatever one's state in life, and obeying God's commandments. That does not mean, however, that the vows of poverty, obedience and chastity are not essential to religious life. Our vows have everything to do with the daily observance of consecrated celibacy. They invite us to demonstrate by our lives that God is our only focus, and that God shapes the expression of our human passions. Observance of our vows becomes a way of life, reflecting our relationship with God.

According to Bianchi, consecrated celibacy is the most specific element of religious life. However, life in community is essentially related to consecrated celibacy. By devoting ourselves exclusively to God, we separate ourselves from our families of origin. We open ourselves to all people, especially the members of our religious families or the people we serve.

Consecrated celibacy includes two other aspects: the prophetic and the eschatological. According to Metz, religious life is always focused on the anticipation of Jesus' return. That eschatological dimension makes us look at reality in a fundamentally different way, placing people and reality in a different perspective. Religious want to proclaim Jesus' return through our lives, showing what the kingdom will be like. In the words of Teresa of Avila, "God alone is enough." This eschatological perspective also makes religious prophetic, since they make God present in the world. They live in the presence of Christ and they bear witness to this presence in their very lives.

In an attempt to summarize this reflection on the identity of religious life, we could say that the most specific feature is consecrated celibacy lived within community. Focused on God and the kingdom, we choose to dedicate our lives to that reality. We receive a special charism that helps us to live devoted to God and focused on the new life heralded by the resurrection. It becomes a life lived in God's reality whereby we meet God in everything and everyone, making religious prophets in our day. Bianchi calls religious life a life of constant conversion whereby our passions are purified and converted by observing vows of chastity, poverty and obedience.[16]

By observing our vows we create a space for a special kind of solidarity with the poor, with those who do not marry, and those who are deprived of their freedom. Metz refers to this as the political consequence of our vows. At the same time, consecrated celibacy creates a new bond with the community. We become the brother or sister of everyone, of those with whom we share our daily lives, with whom we work, and whom we serve in our ministry.

All the faithful are called to a life of holiness by loving God and by loving their neighbours as themselves (Mark 12:29-31). Married people respond to this call by contributing to the continuation of creation, whereas religious live this call by contributing to the realization of the resurrection. Creation needs to be reminded of the resurrection; our origins must remain focused on our final destiny. Both types of vocations are complementary, requiring each other to fully grasp reality. We are no longer talking about superiority, radicalism, opposites or comparisons; we are talking in terms of complementary.

Practical consequences

Consecrated life can be described as searching, seeing and bearing witness to God. These efforts involve a passionate commitment to our fellow human beings. (This passionate commitment may also include prayer and making sacrifices for the well-being of others.) A number of practical implications emerge from this commitment: an openness to new life, the places where we minister, the difference between contemplative and apostolic communities, and the role of the different spiritualities.

Openness to new life

If our charism and consecrated life are rooted in the gospel and in our search for God, we will remain open to and pray for new life. In this way, religious orders and congregations will continue to be a service to the community. Our communities will be places where people can fulfill their call. Young people continue to knock on our doors, showing that religious life is still significant. They hope to find, at the heart of our community, a place where they can fulfill their vocation and their mission in life.

Some groups have not welcomed new members for some time. God, however, still grants them the charism to start anew with one person. There are many examples of congregational charisms that were kept alive by only a handful of religious, and that started to flourish again and lead to new directions. Moreover, a new member may be the refounder who brings new life to the congregation.

We must not too quickly state that it is irresponsible to accept new people in our congregations. The Dutch campaign "Recruit or Perish" convinced many congregations to stop investing in recruitment, leading them to throw in the towel. However, one of those congregations reconsidered its decision a few years later and began new attempts to recruit members, volunteers and staff. Candidates applied in all three categories and some people eventually made a commitment.

Places where we minister

Our passion for God must always lead to a passion for humanity. How can that passion for humanity be expressed? As consecrated people we need to show how God fulfills us, helping others in their search for the deeper meaning of life. Through how we live, what we say and what we do, consecrated people are to demonstrate that God is the only answer to all life's questions and that all other answers – as authentic as they may seem – remain superficial and incomplete. Religious try to put into practice what Teresa of Avila writes:

> Let nothing trouble you; Let nothing frighten you
> Everything passes; God never changes
> Patience Obtains all
> Whoever has God Wants for nothing
> God alone is enough.[17]

Consecrated people must be salt and yeast wherever God's presence is questioned. There is nowhere in the world where religious cannot witness to God's love. Some religious tend to wrap themselves up in a religious subculture, avoiding places where God's message needs to be proclaimed. Religious must remain engaged in the world, supporting all the good that is happening and denouncing all that is evil. Religious must respect and defend gospel values, witnessing to God's love wherever freedom is threatened and compassion is lacking. We see these values in traditional apostolic activities, such as education and health care. Religious need to be involved as salt and yeast, in service to all humanity, in all society's activities.

Consecrated people need to bear witness to the universal humanity wherever they live and work. Through their community life they need to show that the young and the old, the learned and the illiterate can live together.

In places where they live in intercultural communities, religious should speak out against all forms of discrimination.

Their communities should be places where people can recover from traumatic events in their lives, where they can find support, where they can experience new forms of community life, and where they can live in collaboration with others.

The difference between contemplative and apostolic communities

During the Synod on Consecrated Life, many were surprised to learn that the Orthodox church has only one type of religious community. This is in stark contrast with the Roman Catholic church, where there is a distinction between contemplative and apostolic communities and where a great variety of charisms have led to the creation of an equally great variety of separate communities.

Is it helpful to make such a distinction between contemplative and apostolic communities? Is the distinction based on important differences? After all, every consecrated life embraces both contemplative (passion for God) as well as apostolic (passion for humanity) dimensions.

If contemplative life were simply a withdrawal from the world in order to cultivate our own relationship with God, then the contemplative life is an empty shell of what it ought to be. Love of God must always include love of our neighbour. Love of our neighbour can be expressed in different ways, but it will always be situated between the love of all (God appears in whoever we meet, and we are invited to love God in that person) and our preferential option for the poor and the outcast as a concrete expression of Jesus' teaching: "Truly I tell you, just as you did it to one of the least of these who are members of my family, you did it to me" (Matthew 25:40). Love of our neighbour can shape our prayers for a specific neighbour in distress, or for the world at large, also.

If our apostolic life is not based on contemplation, our apostolic activities will amount to little more than social work since they will lack the radical call of Christian charity. Only by searching for God do we find humans – children of God – an icon of Christ and a temple of the Holy Spirit.

Vincent de Paul (1581–1660) developed the basic principle of "abandoning God for God." He says, "If someone calls upon you while you are praying and asks you to help a poor person most urgently, then interrupt your praying, or rather continue your praying. For in that case, you are abandoning God for God. If you go out to visit the poor ten times a day, you are sure to meet God ten times a day too."[18]

Mother Teresa showed, through her dedication to the poor, her response to Jesus' words on the cross, "I am thirsty." She understood that we could respond to Jesus' final request only if we had answered his previous request: "Stay awake with me." In her words, "The more we receive in silent prayer, the more we can give in our active life." Were Vincent de Paul and Mother Teresa contemplative or apostolic religious?

New groups catch our attention because of the importance that they give to both contemplation and apostolic life. Perhaps apostolic religious could be invited to lead a more contemplative life, and contemplative religious invited to pay more attention to the apostolic aspect. Otherwise both groups risk becoming empty shells of what they claim to be.

The role of the different spiritualities

As mentioned earlier, Orthodox consecrated life has one single charism, while Roman Catholic consecrated life has many charisms. These multiple charisms have led to the creation of many orders and congregations, each having their own spirituality.

What is so distinctive about these spiritualities? Some are based on the message of God's love and Jesus' commandment to love one's neighbour, while emphasizing specific aspects of that message and that commandment. However, all orders and congregations must ensure that they remain true to the whole gospel message, the contemplative aspect as well as the apostolic.

A number of congregations are characterized by a spirituality that focuses on a particular concern of Jesus – his attention for children or the sick, and his relationship with God. Those congregations must not limit their spirituality to one particular aspect of Jesus' ministry, significant as it may be. Their specific spirituality needs to be grounded within the gospel message as a whole.

Others have a spirituality that is connected to a particular devotion: for example, the devotion to the Sacred Heart. Those devotions are always time-conditioned and must be reviewed in light of today's reality. For example, the devotion to the Sacred Heart can be interpreted as the love of Jesus for all people.

Still other congregations are linked with a particular saint: for example, Joseph, Mary or Gabriel. They, too, need to adapt the strengths of their patron saint for today's world.

Finally, there are groups with long-standing traditions that were named after their founders: Benedict, Augustine, Dominic, Francis, Ignatius, Vincent. They are the large traditional religious families. We need to ask: When does a movement become limited to a unique spirituality, and what keeps a movement at the level of a devotion or a series of devotions?

To my mind, spirituality must always be shaped by gospel values, trying to concretize, radicalize and realize the gospel message. Spirituality should offer a framework that shapes our search for God and helps us follow Jesus.

And then …?

Seeing the future of consecrated life as a challenge sounds positive, and should encourage us to continue to reflect critically. It is an invitation to study the truth of consecrated life and the various ways in which people live it. Once we have defined religious life, we should test our own way of life against it. It is also an invitation to not give up too quickly, to not apply the *ars moriendi* as a premature euthanasia. Some religious groups already hold a defeatist attitude, projecting themselves into a future when there will be no reason to continue. Where is their hope, and what has happened to their faith? Consecrated life as such will never disappear. As an essential vocation in the church, it is important to continue to reflect on the future of consecrated life.

Consecrated life is one way in which people can express their vocation in life. In the next chapter I will consider the specific vocation that shapes religious life. I get a new perspective when I visit other countries and observe the enthusiasm of consecrated people there. We must be prepared to learn from other cultures, and from history. There have been times in our history when the future of consecrated life was as dark as it seems today. But how many new movements, created within those times of crisis, eventually flourished?

Having reflected on the truth of consecrated life, I would like to examine pastoral care of vocations and consider new, emerging associations. On this Easter Saturday, with the experience of Good Friday behind us, we look forward with hope.

4

Our Vows

There are many different paths in life that can lead to fulfillment. Everyone must find and follow their own unique path.

I attended the funeral of a brother who died in an accident. Two years earlier he had left for Africa for the first time, filled with enthusiasm. At his funeral I read an *in memoriam* card; it said "Every person approaches God differently." We need to understand "approaches God differently" in more than the context of death. We "approach God" throughout the course of our lives as God walks a unique journey with each one of us.

There are a number of paths by which we can draw nearer to God, or along which we can walk in God's company. The path that religious or consecrated people choose is but one of those paths. It is not a better path than the path of marriage, priesthood or committed laity. However, it is a specific and unique path that we pursue within a certain framework: the framework of evangelical counsels and religious vows.

We follow the path of consecrated life, as a path to full life, to the extent that we observe the vows that come with consecrated life. In fact, our vows help us to stay on the path of consecrated life. I would first like to explain what the path of consecrated life is, and then explain the framework – the vows – more specifically.

Consecrated life

The document *Vita Consecrata* states that "the evangelical basis of consecrated life is to be sought in the special relationship which Jesus, in his earthly life, established with some of his disciples" (14). This refers to the story of the transfiguration on Mount Tabor, where Jesus went with three of his disciples: Peter, John and James. These were the same disciples whom he would later ask to accompany him to the garden at Gethsemane. On Mount Tabor the disciples heard God say, "This is my Son, the Beloved; listen to him!" (Mark 9:7); in the garden Jesus asked them, "Remain here, and stay awake with me" (Matthew 26:38). Were these three disciples better than the others who had not been invited? No, but Jesus had chosen them; this was their specific mission or vocation.

The vocation to live a consecrated life is similar: God chooses some people with whom to establish a more intense relationship. It is a mystery (to which only God holds the key) why God specifically chooses certain people. It is up to those people to accept God's invitation, or not.

In *The Fire in These Ashes,* Joan Chittister writes, "Religious must be the person who first and foremost, always and forever, in whatever circumstance, seeks God and God alone, sees God and God alone in all of this confusion, in all of this uncertainty and, whatever the situation, speaks God – and God alone."[19] In other words, being a religious implies seeking, seeing and bearing witness to God in every aspect of life, and in all circumstances. There is something very passionate about that: passionately seeking, seeing and bearing witness to God because God seeks, sees and loves us passionately. We can say that religious people are passionate people on account of their personal relationship with God and with Jesus. God's own passion for humankind is contagious and infuses us all. Johann Baptist Metz also describes contemporary religious life as "a passion for God."[20]

Religious passionately desire that God's justice become a reality in our lives, the lives of others and the whole world. We devote ourselves entirely to that call in a passionate way. This explains why the passion for God always includes a passion for humankind. Mysticism, or passion for God, should always lead to politics, or passion for people. Metz puts that very pertinently: "The church is not primarily a moral institution but rather a passer-on of certain expectations. And its theology is not primarily an ethic but rather an eschatology."[21] It is precisely that eschatology that generates an ethic of not postponing those expectations until the hereafter, but giving them a place right now.

Similarly, consecrated life is a passionate search for God in answer to God's passionate search for humankind. We realize that the eventual union with God can take place only in the hereafter, but we nevertheless try to anticipate it in our own lives, and also in the lives of others. We wish to inform others that God loves them as well, and we want to show that by helping to improve their life situation, by bringing them the joy of the resurrection here and now.

This passion for God, this passionate search for God, has an impact on the lives of all who wish to live a consecrated life. Religious make our own passions inferior to the passion for God, which will eventually dominate all other passions. God comes first, and the individual and personal passions are orientated towards the passion for God. The passionate side of our personality is not so much repressed, as people used to say, as given a new focus: a life fulfillment that has everything to do with God.

Note that the passion for God is a mutual passion. God has a passion for us as well!

All who are called to live a consecrated life, and who heed the call, make God the one and only, and most profound fulfillment of their lives. For God contains everything and all. The religious put all their strength, their abilities – their whole being – in their search for God and their desire to live in God's presence. This searching demonstrates what awaits us in the future (the eschatological dimension of consecrated life). Religious show the world that things will find their right place only in relationship with God (the prophetic dimension of consecrated life). They deal differently with reality, which becomes where we find God and where God's love becomes visible, even in the lives of people who are hurt (the apostolic dimension of consecrated life). Religious live together with others, following the example of the first Christians who were full of Jesus' presence in their midst (the communal dimension of consecrated life). They become extremely sensitive to those places where God weeps, and where people are wounded as a consequence of the divine obfuscation (the liminal dimension of consecrated life).

Chittister writes, "For the religious, immersion in God becomes the single, unmitigated and unnuanced reason for making every other plausible, worthy and determining motive in life – love, money, children, personal success – secondary to the life pursuit of mystery among us. Immersion in God is the concept that brooks no other greater than itself. That is why our love must be first and foremost a spiritual quest."[22] A consecrated person is primarily a spiritual being.

What passions should be directed to the realization of God's passion? They are the passion for power, the passion for pleasure, and the passion for property. Human life is aimed at the gratification of those three passions: humans want to have power over others and control over all situations; humans want to enjoy life; and humans want to possess the world. It is precisely those passions that are addressed by the religious vows and the evangelical counsels, and become channelled into passion for God. The vow of chastity channels our passion for pleasure; the vow of obedience channels our passion for power; and the vow of poverty channels our passion for property. The vows become the framework within which we shape consecrated life. Let us study that framework in more detail.

In the light of freedom

There is a danger of understanding our vows as the suppression of passion. In that case, the vow of chastity would imply the suppression of one's sexual desire, the vow of poverty the suppression of the desire to accumulate material wealth, and the vow of obedience the suppression of the desire for power.

It is true that our vows have something to do with the renunciation or rejection of the dominant aspect of our passions. But we must not give the last word to pleasure, power or property because there is something bigger, infinitely bigger: our passion for God and God's passion for us. But the passion for pleasure, power or property needs be addressed. The fact that we refuse to give our passions the last word does not mean that our passions must be eliminated entirely.

Our goal is not to control our passions completely (trying to suppress our passions means that they will likely emerge in other forms), but to give them expression within our deep passion for God. It is strange to speak of our passion for God while ignoring our natural passions. The only way to seek and love God passionately is through our natural passions. It is how we can love God while respecting our human nature with all our hearts, our minds and our abilities. Otherwise, our love of God, in answer to God's passion for us, cannot be passionate. It will be purely spiritual. Then we find ourselves in a dualism that divides us into a spiritual component and a physical component. The religious aspect is pushed into the spiritual corner, causing us to think that our body has nothing to do with religion. And yet Jesus showed through his incarnation that religion is not purely spiritual but involves us as a whole. As the incarnation of God, Jesus was concerned about humans as a whole: spirit and body, spirit and passion! The renunciation of the body, based on the belief that it was an impediment for those wanting to live a spiritual life, is the result of the dualism that existed for several centuries. Religious vows were intended to mortify the flesh, the physical part of our existence, based in a very negative understanding of the body. Did God create something dirty, something negative in creating our bodies? Do we not approach God with our spirit *and* our body? Do we not speak of our body as the temple of the Holy Spirit?

Today, when we make our vows we understand them as an invitation to orientate our passions towards our passion for God, and God's passion for us. The desires for power, material wealth and pleasure are a reality in each person's life. They are the great forces of life, the life forces! The goal is to eliminate their violent aspect, their dominance, the power they have over us, the power of making us slaves of our own passions, in order to channel them into life forces that fulfill our lives: the passion for God, and God's passion for us.

The Good News states that, in the end, our only possession is God, our only desire is God. We wish to orientate our lives completely towards God. We will study this in more detail by discussing the three specific vows.

Unmarried for the kingdom

Augustine wrote, "Virginity is the uninterrupted and constant meditation on the resurrection as long as I am still in my mortal body."[23] He establishes a tone by which we should interpret the vow of virginity: unmarried for the kingdom of heaven.

Today, three words are used to describe this vow: chastity, celibacy and purity. The vow of purity implies dealing *purely* with our passion for pleasure. Virginity is more an attitude to life that allows us to stay open to everyone without becoming attached to one person in particular. Celibacy is the unmarried state in life: remaining unmarried, voluntarily or involuntarily. In other words, celibacy is a state in life, virginity or chastity an attitude to life, and purity the virtuous way in which we deal with our passion for pleasure. Purity as a virtue is not strictly reserved for those who have opted for virginity or celibacy in life; everyone is called to be pure in their state in life and attitude to life. When we speak about the vow of purity as religious, we interpret it in combination with chastity and celibacy.

Augustine wrote that our vows need to be interpreted in light of the resurrection. They are a way of living as resurrected beings, within the promise of the resurrection. Consecrated life in its eschatological dimension is an anticipation of the life that awaits us.

It is the same with the vow of purity. It becomes meaningful only if we interpret it in the context of the promise of the resurrection, our passion for God and God's passion for us, and the desire to belong entirely to God. To do that we must refine our passions – in this case, the passion for pleasure – purify them to free ourselves of selfishness and violence, and orientate ourselves towards the coming of the kingdom and a full relationship with God. The energy contained in the passion for pleasure must not be suppressed but instead channelled.

The vow of purity is all about the purification of human love, situating it within the primacy of divine love as it is defined in the commandment to love God and our neighbour as ourselves. Ignatius of Loyola said, "Give me your love, that is enough." Teresa of Avila cried out, "God alone is enough." The Apostle Paul said, "Neither death, nor life ... nor anything else in all creation will be able to separate us from the love of God" (Rom 8:39).

The first step is to make our passions subordinate to God's love, God's passion. Our passion – call it our affection – can no longer have the last word; it must serve love as expressed in the commandment of love. Then we will look upon God, our neighbour and ourselves in a purely emotional and affectionate way. We will look upon humankind and the world from God's point of view, dealing with them inspired by God's loving commitment. Friendship is important because it is a consequence of our love of the other.

Friendship, in consecrated life, is good and even necessary, insofar as we do not lay claim to our friends, or use them to fight feelings of emptiness. In doing so friendship becomes perverted. It is important to ask: Is my desire to be with my friend pure? Is the way I look upon my friend pure?

Our understanding of sexuality must be situated within this tension: while we wish to express ourselves in an affectionate and emotional way, there is always the risk of laying claim to the other person. Sexuality is a positive force as long as it upholds the humanity of the other, and our own humanity from an affective point of view. But any sexual behaviour that is egotistic or abuses others for our own pleasure distances us from the positive features of sexuality.

It is entirely possible to become attracted to aspects of the body but things start going wrong as soon as we start using it for our own ego's pleasure. That is why trust and caution should go hand in hand in the context of purity. We should deal truthfully and positively with our passion, with our sexuality, with our affections, while realizing that we need to be careful because there is always the danger of our ego taking over. It is important that we remain honest with ourselves. Anything that does not bring us closer to God, or that drives us away from God, must be avoided. Suppression is not the right answer; rather, integration in our life project is what we seek. It requires lifelong practice, with the grace of God, to purify ourselves of all that makes us stray from the path to God, the path to pure love. Some say that our ego will disappear in the first hour after our death.

I return to the idea of dealing charitably with the reality in us, and the fact that we know that God knows us and loves us as we are. We can say and pray with the psalmist: "O Lord, you have searched me and known me. You know when I sit down and when I rise up; you discern my thoughts from far away. You search out my path and my lying down, and are acquainted with all my ways" (Psalm 139:1-3). We must be aware that we can hope to purify ourselves, thanks to the grace of God.

Your kingdom come, your will be done

The vow of obedience invites us to purify our passion for power and to invest all our energy in the development of the kingdom of God. Here we must follow in Jesus' footsteps when he said that he had come to fulfill God's will, and that he therefore wished to be a servant. This twofold mission seems to contrast with the power that we wish to develop: satisfy our own will and rule others. In this instance, we are talking about a double shift: not to fulfill my will but the will of God (as it is made known to me through people and situations), and not to rule others but to serve them.

Our power is stripped from its egoism when it serves a higher purpose: that of ushering in the kingdom of God on earth, the well-being of the entire person, our passion for God and God's passion for us, which translates into a passion for all humans.

In each of us there is the tendency to try to take reality, organize it and structure it according to our own vision and beliefs. Society's development is the result of that tendency. We all need an area in which we can realize ourselves and in which we can engage with people and situations. This is a positive thing as long as this power is used well while remaining at the service of the development of society. But when we use our power, evil is waiting around the corner to subvert and to pervert it. Power then becomes a purpose in itself that rules our minds (the mind of the person in power as well as the minds of those around that person). Personal freedom is sacrificed on the altar of power. The striving for power and for more power can become the sole purpose and eventually consume all of a person's energy. History has taught us and still teaches us the disastrous consequences of that tendency. Even in our own lives we experience the struggle that threatens to undermine our positive use of power, thus damaging our freedom. It is because of this constant threat that the use of power becomes abuse of power, resulting in a negative connotation to the word "power."

Even Christ reacted negatively to the abuse of power. He taught that every use of power must be at the service of others. He often repeated, paradoxical though it may seem, that whoever wanted to be the greatest had to become like the little ones, and had to serve the others (Matthew 18:3-4; Mark 9:35; Luke 9:48, 22:26).

The vow of obedience invites us to develop that basic attitude of service. We are invited to help create a community at the service of others. Whenever we make another person subordinate to our personal needs, we stray from the path of service, and we risk abusing our power. The problem is that this can go unnoticed because we blind ourselves with all kinds of good intentions. It becomes ever more dangerous when people are bypassed in favour of an idea, however noble that idea may be. Anyone who becomes a slave to their principles and ideas loses their true freedom, even though they are convinced that these principles and ideas will guarantee and increase their freedom. Eventually the only ones they listen to are themselves, and to those people who contribute to their self-assurance and to their own profit.

The vow of obedience fundamentally contradicts this. When we make that vow we promise to listen more carefully to others and to their questions in order to help them improve their life. From a theological point of view, we want to listen first to God and to what God has to say about humankind and the world. Anthropologically speaking, it implies that we have to devote our entire life project to promoting humanity's well-being. And here, too, something miraculous will happen. If we organize our own life project so that it contributes to the well-being of others, we will have the pleasure of feeling good about our own lives.

Listening is an important part of obedience – listening to God's voice in people and in all situations. It is through them that God speaks to us. Are we receptive to God's message, or do we hear only our own words?

The Bible tells how God speaks through people and certain events. God often asks people to listen: "Listen, my people" (Psalm 50:7, 78:1, 81:8). And on Mount Tabor, at the transfiguration, the three apostles were told, "Listen to him" (Matthew 17:5; Mark 9:7; Luke 9:35).

Obedience is more than simply respecting a set of rules and regulations, or asking permission for whatever we want to do. It is above all recognizing the voice of the living God who invites us to follow him in the concrete events in life and in our relationships with others. Every meeting can be an encounter with God and a sign from God. It is up to us to become attentive to those signs. That is only possible when we open our hearts to everyone we meet. The cry from the oppressed and outcast person is also a cry from God, who cries with his people: "I have observed the misery of my people who are in Egypt; I have heard their cry on account of their taskmasters. Indeed, I know their sufferings" (Exodus 3:7). Filled with God's passion for people, we must fight any injustice that makes God's people suffer. That becomes very active obedience, an obedience that is more than following or respecting certain rules and regulations, rules that often reflect self-made systems that guarantee a secure life. When we seek a safe and secure life, we lose any energy generated by our desire for power. True obedience is aimed at focusing that energy to the well-being of others, and at establishing the kingdom of God on earth.

Obedience also requires trust and caution. Trust because striving for power is not wrong when it serves the well-being of others and the establishment of the kingdom of God: "Your kingdom come." Caution because in that power is contained a lot of ego, blind ambition and the urge to prove oneself, all of which serve personal well-being rather than the well-being of others: "Your will be done." We need to ask if we are fooling ourselves, constantly checking to see if it is God's will that we seek. Similarly, the expression "following one's conscience" can be an excuse to do our own will based on selfish motives because of our ambition and wanting to prove ourselves. Only with God's mercy can we hope to purify our passion for power, day after day.

Becoming poor in heart

Finally, there is the vow of poverty whereby we stop striving for material wealth. Property and ownership are important values that come naturally to humans. In Genesis we were given ownership of the earth and all that it produces, and we were invited to manage it. The ownership of the earth is kept in perspective by its management. We are not owners but privileged users and careful managers. The same distortion that happens with pleasure and power can happen with ownership. From a means of developing our life and that of others, it can become a purpose in itself that can consume all our energy. Eventually, humans find that it is never enough, and they develop an insatiable desire for more. The misery we try to ignore by accumulating material wealth causes new and endless misery: How can I safeguard what I already possess, and add more to it?

The lack of material goods can never be seen as something good. But it is essential to be able to say "enough," and to stick by that decision. The reality of poverty and underdevelopment could be solved if many were to adopt that attitude of enough. Every unnecessary possession implies that others are deprived of something that is essential for them to stay alive. Exploiting nature is also a concern these days. These thoughts are uncomfortable because putting them into practice is painful. The line between what is essential and what is extra is not that clear. Moreover, the same is true for the line between using something and coveting something. The vow of poverty is an invitation to expect everything we need from God, trusting that God will provide.

In a religious community we have the advantage of being free from worrying about material needs. We are given the necessities for life, and so much more. However, we risk growing attached to that worry-free existence, and making it a goal in itself. Our existence becomes based on settling somewhere safe, secure and isolated from the world. This contradicts the gospel call to be ready at all times, to go out, and to devote our entire existence to the well-being of others. The vow of poverty is, apart from an invitation to cultivate that feeling of having enough in our lives, a call to sacrifice ourselves instead of withdrawing. We are called to sacrifice ourselves, using all our talents and abilities to help build God's world for which Jesus gave his life. We are freed from worries about material needs so we can worry only about the coming of the kingdom of God.

The essence of the vow of poverty is related to the way in which we deal with ourselves: as fearful and covetous owners of our life or as peaceful givers of life. As people who are over-concerned about their own health, or as spontaneous people who worry about other people's well-being and health. A consequence of our vow of poverty will be our happiness and joyfulness: happy with what we are given each day, and seeing in it the generous hand of God who gives us all. The vow of poverty is the prefiguration of how we will be one day: no longer attached to any earthly possessions, and completely satisfied with God. Teresa of Avila's expression "God is enough for me" is once again very appropriate.

Religious poverty means being satisfied with what we have, wanting to share what we have, and not being overly concerned about what tomorrow will bring. The Rule of Life of the Brothers of Charity is very clear: "Your time, your talents, the riches of your heart, your engaging goodness, all belong to those who are bereft of such gifts ... Your face radiates the goodness of the Father" (30).

The basic question with regard to the vow of poverty is this: How do we fill our hearts? Will our life be aimed at accumulating possessions, security and achievements, and more of them day after day, or are we capable of distancing ourselves from such material and immaterial goods, relying on God, expecting everything from God who is the only true fulfillment of our lives?

5

Making Room in Our Hearts

Consecrated celibacy is our way of seeking and loving God with all our hearts, with all our minds and with all our inner strength. It is our way of letting God's passion capture us completely. Doing this will alter our lives totally. It will turn us into spiritual people who long for the coming of God in our lives. We become God seekers who cry out with Augustine: "Our hearts are restless until they rest in thee."

Religious life is not something you can simply do on the side, like becoming a member of some association or club. We can say with Paul,

> Yet whatever gains I had, these I have come to regard as loss because of Christ. More than that, I regard everything as loss because of the surpassing value of knowing Christ Jesus my Lord. For his sake I have suffered the loss of all things, and I regard them as rubbish, in order that I may gain Christ and be found in him, not having a righteousness of my own that comes from the law, but one that comes through faith in Christ, the righteousness from God based on faith. (Philippians 3:7-9)

The Rule of Life of the Brothers of Charity also states: "This love of Christ dictates all your actions; you will as it were be captivated by it. This implies that every other love must be integrated in this sole love, giving it a deeper meaning. With God's help and mastery over self, you will reject every threat to this total gift of yourself" (10).

That is quite a challenge; it requires conversion regarding the way we treat ourselves and the way we treat others. The consequences of our undivided devotion to the love of Christ, the coming of the kingdom of God, and the passion of God become apparent on three different levels that also constitute the three dimensions of our consecrated life.

The first dimension is our personal relationship with God, which becomes more and more definitive every day through our prayers. The second dimension is our relationship with the people around us. (There is an extra dimension to this since we live together in communities.) The third and last dimension is our relationship with the world, and our attentiveness to those whose human dignity is threatened or violated. In other words, we are talking about our prayer, our community and our apostolate, which are the expressions of our consecrated life, of the way we seek God and of how passionately we love God.

In this chapter I wish to analyze our prayer life as the expression of our relationship with God, our community life as the expression of our relationship with our fellow humans, and our apostolate as the expression of our concern for the world that surrounds us and in which we live.

Our prayer is that of all Christians who want to open their hearts to God's overwhelming love and want to respond to that love. It is God who takes the initiative; we must open up our hearts in order to welcome God's love. Praying must be preceded by a self-emptying that needs to be our basic attitude. As long as we are full of ourselves, we cannot pray.

Belonging to God

The basis of every religious life is the undivided gift of one's life to God. The core of the vocation to the religious life is the desire to dedicate oneself entirely to God and the willingness to seal this by choosing a life of consecrated celibacy. Religious enter a state of life that redirects them completely and turns them into someone completely new. This redirection or reorientation is given expression when candidates start their novitiate. From that moment on, they are called "brother" or "sister"; in the past they would even receive a new name. As well, they receive the religious habit as an expression of the fundamental change that they have gone through.

At this time they join the congregation, still laden with their personality, background, character and passions. Those cannot be denied or ignored, let alone suppressed. Religious are to accept their reality lovingly, and it is with and from that reality that they walk with Jesus. Their journey will be one of transformation and of constant conversion so they can say, "He must increase but I must decrease" (John 3:30).

In *Vita Consecrata*, religious are called to be contemplative men and women, to behold God's glory in order to be able to recognize God in God's humanity. "The evangelical basis of consecrated life is to be sought in the special relationship which Jesus, in his earthly life, established with some of his disciples. He called them not only to welcome the Kingdom of God into their own lives, but also to put their lives at its service, leaving everything behind and closely imitating his own way of life" (*VC*, 14). In other words, it involves following Jesus more closely and belonging to God in an undivided way.

This undivided gift requires a constant redirection towards God. The only way to achieve this is through contemplation. With some religious, the word "contemplation" brings to mind a return to the pre-conciliar period when most orders prayed often, especially as a community. Over the years, a lot of monastic customs were introduced in the lives of apostolic congregations. The question, however, is whether that led to real contemplation. I still hear some religious referring to spiritual exercises, saying, "Phew, I've done my exercises for today!" Just as we do physical exercises because it is good for our health, some regard spiritual exercises as something that they are obliged to do. It then becomes a matter of doing those exercises as quickly as possible by rattling off a series of prayers and spending the rest of the time reading all sorts of religious literature. When apostolic congregations got rid of those monastic customs after Vatican II and reduced community prayer to a minimum, many religious felt relieved. A lot of those monastic customs had lost all meaning for them. What was supposed to lead to a more contemplative lifestyle no longer did. The rituals remained but that was all they were. (We must be careful about generalizing, for we all know religious who grew into truly contemplative people.) But the fact is that some got rid of the contemplative dimension when they banned the monastic customs from apostolic communities. The baby was thrown out with the bathwater once again.

Community prayer was reduced to a minimum: morning and evening prayers, Eucharist, sometimes a rosary, meditation or spiritual reading. It is important to do those things conscientiously, even if the community is small or made up of elderly religious. However, the mere attendance of such common moments of prayer will not be enough to develop a true contemplative attitude. That requires personal prayer where we spend time with God. Cardinal Bernardin admitted that he always reserved the first hour of the day for the Lord.

> You have to make good quality time for praying, spend the first hour of the day praying. The effect of that first hour will not cease once that hour is over. That hour unites me with the Lord at the beginning of the day, but it also keeps me connected to him for the rest of the day. Even if you do not use that time optimally, you must not spend it on someone else. But if you spend that time on him, you will gradually grow connected to the Lord with your whole life.[24]

Personal prayer is essential for religious who wish to develop that contemplative attitude. Only when they have first beheld the face of God, contemplated it and grown aware of God's presence in their hearts can they discover God in the world. Mother Teresa said, "We can only give a positive reply to Jesus' final outcry on the cross, 'I'm thirsty,' if we have followed him to Gethsemani and have given a positive reply to his request, 'Stay awake with me!'"[25]

Vincent de Paul said that we must discover Christ in the poor. But he said that we first had to meet Christ in the sacrament. This wisdom has been passed on to us by people who show us how their entire lives are rooted in an intense prayer life. Cardinal Nguyên Vân Thuân spent several years in a prison in Vietnam and had nothing and no one to fall back upon. That extreme experience taught him what it meant to really choose God and not God's works. His challenge is that we must first choose God, and do so in reality, and not stick to devout spiritual thoughts. It is tempting to seek certainty in our activities and our relationships and to live in the illusion that we are doing everything we can for God. The disillusionment will not come until our work is taken from us and we have no relationships on which to fall back: we have only ourselves to rely on. Then do we fall into the arms of God, or into a void? Real spiritual people who can say in all honesty that they require nothing else but God have no fear about losing their jobs or their health. As Etty Hillesum said while she was imprisoned in a concentration camp, "They can take away everything. They can even take my life, but they can never steal my God."[26] Often religious, both individually and as a group, are overly preoccupied with the works of God, believing that those works represent God. "God first and the works will follow. But sometimes they will not and then we will have to manage with God alone," says Nguyên Vân Thuân.[27]

Mary held a similar attitude after the annunciation. She gave up her quiet life and abandoned all her plans to rely solely on the word of the Lord. "Fiat," she replied, and the miracle of the incarnation could take place. No wonder Mary is considered the ultimate model for religious. She invites them to follow her example by giving the most prominent place in her life to God; by belonging to God in an undivided way and by spending the best of time with God in prayer. There is no middle road. The mission, the life mission of every religious, is to belong entirely to God, with all that it entails. It is the basis of our lives that must be given the highest priority.

With Jesus

Vita Consecrata describes the religious' relationship with Jesus: "These Religious are called to be brothers of Christ, deeply united with him, 'the firstborn among many brothers'" (*VC*, 60).

Religious are invited to develop an intense and intimate relationship with Jesus as their closest brother. Many among us are not used to dealing intimately with Jesus. We pray to a remote, transcendent God whom we address as Lord God, Almighty, or Father in heaven. The transcendent is one dimension of God, but through the incarnation, God has shown us how immanent he is, also. God is distant and close, almighty and merciful. Praying has to do with opening up to the God who wishes to live deep in our hearts. It is getting to the point that we no longer see God as an object but as a subject. When we become aware of that presence, we no longer strive to know *about* God; we strive for a more profound relationship *with* God. This is an important step in our relationship with God: to realize that God is present in our lives and to open up to God's love. It is also the start of all prayer: to open up to God's presence and to say with our hearts and minds, "Yes, God, you are there and you are there with your love of me." Prayer is standing in front of God with all of our reality.

Abraham Joshua Heschel explains this quite strikingly in his book *Man's Quest for God*:

> Having realized that we are a mixture of modesty and insolence, of self-denial and self-delusion, we beg God to save us. We ask him to help us to become master of our own thoughts, words and actions. We put all our strength before him. To pray is to end up on that frontier. In prayer, the core of our lives is shifted from self-awareness to self-sacrifice. God becomes the centre around which all other forces circle.[28]

Placing ourselves in the presence of God is not fully prayer, but it is a good start. It is necessary to adopt this basic attitude so that God's Spirit might become active in us. Paul is very clear about this: "Likewise the Spirit helps us in our weakness; for we do not know how to pray as we ought, but that very Spirit intercedes with sighs too deep for words" (Romans 8:26). We should start every prayer by putting ourselves in the presence of God and by asking God to let the Spirit pray in us. Prayer requires a reversal of our human standard of values: shifting the centre of our lives that lies within us to God. It means replacing our activity by passive openness, and our speaking with silence and a willingness to listen.

God is present in us in the Trinity. As creator, God wants to be reborn in us time and again. God wants to enter our humanity with all his divinity, sending us the Spirit to inspire us. Are we really conscious of the Trinity or do we pray exclusively to the Father, or to Jesus or to the Holy Spirit? When we make the sign of the cross, we place ourselves within the Trinity, asking that we speak, act and think in the name of the Father, Son and Holy Spirit. As religious, we address ourselves to God in our prayers as though we were his children and he were our Father: a Father whom we look to with respect, to whom we are willing to listen and who we know loves us unconditionally. We know our Father as the origin of our existence and our ultimate destination, who calls us and who sends us. We do not mind going to the Father to ask for protection, for forgiveness and especially for love. Being God's children we can approach Jesus as our brother. He is the one who shares our humanity. By experience he knows our pain but also our joys. That creates an enormous feeling of solidarity. We look to Jesus as our big brother, as an example. When we reflect on his words and actions, we are invited to identify ourselves with him. We recognize ourselves in the disciples who were invited to become Jesus' brothers in faith. Just like them, we try to follow Jesus, though at times we find it difficult to understand him and feel inclined to run from him back to our boats. When we deny him we must face whether we really love him more than anyone or anything in the world.

We receive Jesus in the Eucharist over and over; he approaches us as no other person has ever approached us. He becomes one with us. We experience Jesus' brotherly love in the Eucharist. For religious, the Jesus Prayer can facilitate uninterrupted praying, permitting us to join Jesus in an even more intimate fashion. "Lord Jesus Christ, Son of God, have mercy on me, a sinner" becomes a mantra that brings our hearts closer to God while we are at work, resting or relaxing. It is an unending request for forgiveness based on the realization that without God's constant forgiveness and grace, life is impossible. The Jesus Prayer makes it possible for grace to be born out of weakness, as Paul suggests. It is when we stop trying to keep everything under control ourselves that we give God the chance to let his grace do its healing work. Indeed, God is at the door to our hearts and is knocking quietly. But there is no door handle on the outside; the door can only be opened by us from the inside. That is what the Jesus Prayer does: it opens the door to our hearts in order to let God enter.

As Jesus' brothers and sisters, we were given his mother as our defender. "Here is your mother" (John 19:27), Jesus said on the cross to John and to us all. As Jesus' brothers and sisters, we may approach his (and our) mother and ask her to take us to him and to bring him to us. As we pray the rosary, we browse, with Mary, through the photo album of Jesus' life and reflect on his death and resurrection. It is a contemplative prayer that deepens our relationship with Jesus. It is Mary who introduces us to her son and our brother: "through Mary to Jesus."

Religious bear witness to the fact that their intimate relationship with Jesus in prayer eventually allows them to meet Jesus in every person. Meeting with Jesus in prayer is extended to our meeting Jesus in the world. That is taking the call to pray constantly seriously!

Listening to God's will

"Then his mother and his brothers came to him, but they could not reach him because of the crowd. And he was told, 'Your mother and your brothers are standing outside, wanting to see you.' But he said to them, 'My mother and my brothers are those who hear the word of God and do it'" (Luke 8:19-21). By his reply Jesus indicated what he expected from his brothers and sisters. Just like his mother, they were to listen to the word of God and act on it. It is remarkable that Jesus put his brothers and sisters in the same position as his mother. He knew that his mother possessed the right attitude, since she had organized her entire life according to what God expected of her. In that passage, Jesus asks the same of all those who call themselves his brothers and sisters. This creates new ties. The narrow family ties are abandoned in favour of ties based solely on whether one is prepared to follow Jesus. In order to listen to the word of God, one must read it, contemplate it and give it a place in one's life. That is the age-old *lectio divina* that was developed by the monks as a type of contemplation. Through the centuries, the *lectio divina* was replaced by meditation, which is more of an intellectual activity, an exercise whereby one explores the Word of God and draws conclusions with regard to one's own life.

Meditation, as we have known it since Ignatius, has its merits, but it is merely an introduction to contemplation. Every attempt to listen to the Word of God starts with meditation but should result in contemplation, whereby the Word of God comes alive in our hearts and is expressed in our lives. Enzo Bianchi says that *lectio divina* is a real way of losing one's life (see Mark 8:35) for the Lord, whereby the gospel becomes reality in our lives.[29]

Lectio divina can be summarized in four words: *lectio*, *meditatio*, *oratio* and *contemplatio*. Before starting the *lectio divina* it is necessary to observe a moment of silence to create an attentive inner space. Concentration is needed to dwell on a passage. It is contrary to all current trends, for today everything moves at high speed: texts are read only diagonally, vocabulary is reduced to a few terms and abbreviations. Today words have become empty; they have been stripped of all meaning and value. "In the beginning was the Word, and the Word was with God, and the Word was God" (John 1:1), we read in the gospel. But Genesis also starts with God's word: "Then God said, 'Let there be light'; and there was light" (Genesis 1:3). And the bible ends with a word from God: "The one who testifies to these things says, '"Surely I am coming soon.' Amen. Come, Lord Jesus!'" (Revelation 22:20).

Lectio divina involves dealing differently with words, valuing them as the ultimate means of expression for humankind and of divinity in the Bible. God comes to us through the word, and we come to know God's will.

The first step in *lectio divina* is reading the Word of God. We are asked to read the text attentively, quietly, and to repeat it several times. The liturgy offers us the opportunity to know the main texts of the Bible over the years. The daily reading of the liturgical texts is, therefore, a good way to start the *lectio divina*.

Reading is followed by meditation or reflection, dealing with the text at an intellectual level. With the help of biblical commentaries, we try to understand the full depth of the text. According to the Ignatian method, we need to use all our senses to imagine what the persons and the surroundings looked like and sounded like. That leads us to try to understand what God is saying to us today through the text. We can end our meditation by examining our conscience, by holding our own life against the message in the text.

Next comes *oratio*, or praying. Having listened attentively (*lectio*) and reflected thoroughly (*meditatio*), the time is right to respond to God's invitation and challenge understood in the Holy Spirit. It becomes a prayer of praise and thanksgiving, and a plea for help. Our self-awareness grows into self-sacrifice. This represents a shift from the mind to the heart, without denying the mind, however. We pray with our whole being, not just with our minds or our emotions. As we pray, our hearts and minds become one, and God becomes present in our full humanity.

Our praying becomes contemplation when we are silent and open ourselves to God's love. We look at God with our hearts full of love and let God shower us with love. We say confidently: "Yes, God, You are there for me, with your love!" It is truly the Holy Spirit who prays in us, who makes God present in our lives, who allows God's grace to become fertile in our lives. Here we become one with God's will, which we heard and on which we meditated and for which we prayed. This is where the Holy Spirit offers her fruits, "love, joy, peace, patience, kindness, generosity, faithfulness, gentleness, and self-control" (Galatians 5:22-23). Those are the fruits of *lectio divina* that God wants to see in our lives.

6

United in God

Over the past few years, many people have thought and written about community. Everyone agrees that humans are social beings. Humans become fully human through their relationships with others. At the same time, we notice how difficult it is to form a community, especially the more permanent forms of community, such as marriage or religious life.

Young people today are afraid of committing themselves for life, and are choosing longer periods of what I call "temporary-ness" before making a definitive choice. Many leave or withdraw from the community they had joined at an earlier stage.

There are many different types of communities. We all want to be a member of one or another group or club. We all belong to a work or recreational community; the bond with one community is often stronger than with another. To become a member of a group or community often we have to pay a membership fee, while other groups or communities expect us to attend meetings and participate in certain activities.

In religious life there are various kinds of communities, too. An abbey is a totally different type of community from an apostolic congregation, and even between two different apostolic congregations there can be a large number of differences.

Every community has its own characteristics. They develop from certain traditions, from certain informal agreements within the community, and especially as a result of the people who are part of the community.

We are all familiar with the range from less hospitable to more welcoming communities. Sometimes one person can influence the entire atmosphere in the community, for better or for worse.

Is community life essential for religious life? Hermits were, and still are, considered religious, and they do not need to live in community to be able to direct all their attention to God. The desert monks started living together for practical reasons; they drew up rules for specific purposes, but they did not pay much attention to the quality of their community life.

The Rule of Augustine, which started as a specific kind of shared living, is an exception, and gives priority to the life of the community. With the introduction of the Rule of Benedict, the importance of community life was emphasized, although the monk was still considered a hermit. The Rule stresses the importance of solitude and silence, rather than community and dialogue.

But let us leave history for now and consider how religious live in community today.

Religious community

When we talk about religious community, we are talking about a community of faith. Faith is the essence of a religious community. Communities were created when people decided to live together because of their shared vision on faith and their common understanding of the gospel message.

The Bible offers various models of communities based on faith. We have the example of Jesus, who established a community with his apostles. They gave up their day-to-day activities in order to follow him. They listened to his invitation to love each other, and saw how he washed their feet as an example of what it meant to serve others.

The Acts of the Apostles contains many references to the first Christian communities (see Acts 2:44-47 and Acts 4:31-35). These texts can be interpreted in different ways. Augustine, who used these texts as the basis for his Rule and for his own community life, provides us with four different interpretations. He stresses the importance of being united, heart and soul: "Now the whole group of those who believed were of one heart and soul" (Acts 4:32). In a second interpretation he emphasizes the importance of common ownership: "No one claimed private ownership of any possessions, but everything they owned was held in common" (Acts 4:32). He saw common ownership as a form of freedom from material concerns. The passage can also be interpreted as an invitation to encourage love as the rule of the community. According to Augustine, it is impossible to talk about a community if its members do not truly love each other. Finally, this passage can be interpreted from a more apostolic point of view: the community must not remain isolated but be open to the world through service to the church.

Those four interpretations are complementary. Every one of them says something fundamental about community life: a feeling of unity, common ownership, reciprocal love, and openness.

We find another model in Matthew, more specifically in this phrase: "For where two or three are gathered in my name, I am there among them" (Matthew 18:20). This confirms how important it is to form a community in order to welcome Christ in our midst.

In the description of a religious community, Psalm 133:1 is often quoted: "How very good and pleasant it is when kindred live together in unity!"

All these texts contain an eschatological reference: the religious community here on earth is seen as an anticipation of the heavenly community. Every religious community is first and foremost a gathering with Jesus at its centre. The bond between the religious always passes through the centre that is Christ. This is what makes the religious community fundamentally different from a secular community where people gather together around a certain project. In a religious community, Christ is the cause and purpose of the foundation of the community. All our reflections on religious community must start with that reality.

Loving one another

The cornerstone of every society is mutual respect and love. Respect and love go hand in hand and enrich one another constantly. It is difficult to determine the link between them for they can be both cause and consequence.

In the gospel message everything is centred on love. Paul offers a clear summary of love: "If I speak in the tongues of mortals and of angels, but do not have love, I am a noisy gong or a clanging cymbal. And if I have prophetic powers, and understand all mysteries and all knowledge, and if I have all faith, so as to remove mountains, but do not have love, I am nothing" (1 Corinthians 13:1-2). He also referred to the commandment of love, mentioned in the Old Testament and made real in Jesus: "You shall love the Lord your God with all your heart, and with all your soul, and with all your strength, and with all your mind; and your neighbour as yourself ... do this, and you will live" (Luke 10:27-28).

The basic elements of this commandment to love can be found in the Old Testament, in the laws and prophets (see Matthew 22:40). The Law said, "You shall love the Lord your God with all your heart, and with all your soul, and with all your might" (Deuteronomy 6:5). And the prophets never stopped appealing to people to love their neighbour (James 2:8; Ezekiel 18:5-9; Tobit 4:16-17). But Jesus took that commandment to another level by giving absolute priority to the commandment to love. The radical – indeed, even shocking – character of love became more challenging with the invitation to love our enemy: "You have heard that it was said, 'You shall love your neighbour and hate your enemy.' But I say to you, 'Love your enemies and pray for those who persecute you'" (Matthew 5:43-44). Thus Jesus shows that the love of one's neighbour is fundamentally different from friendship, which has more to do with emotions. It is hard to accept a commandment to become friends with someone. Friendship is something that befalls us. No commandment is needed to tell us to become friends. The situation is totally different, however, when it comes to the love of one's neighbour excluding no one, not even one's worst enemies. To make that possible a commandment is required, because that is beyond our human strength. But is that commandment applicable? To love one's neighbour is an impossible task when it remains isolated from the love of God and the love of friends. Only through the grace of God can we hope to love our neighbour, and only through the support from our good friends are we psychologically able to fulfill that commandment. The love of others should be inspired by the grace of God and enabled by our friendship with others.

This says something fundamental about the love that we are invited to develop in our respective communities. It is not the work of humans alone, for only the unconditional love of God can enable us and give us the strength and grace to love as God does: unconditionally, without measure, without expecting love in return – simply giving love. Without a deep spiritual life, without prayer and without constant conversion, we might be better not to start at all, for we get into dead-end situations caused by our differences. Only when we try to meet Jesus in our confreres and sisters can we love Jesus in them. It is the love of Jesus that we receive as we pray that animates our relationships with our confreres and sisters. That does not become an unworldly spirituality, but a spirituality that is rooted in real life. That does not mean that we should see prayer and spiritual life as the only way in which we can survive the world. Prayer, spiritual life and the love of God are ends in themselves. We wish to love God because God is there for us with his love. "God is the reason why we love God," Bernard of Clairvaux would say.

Contemplation is something pure. It means opening up to God's endless love and, in return, loving God unconditionally. If this happens, then our love will not remain restricted to prayers alone, but will have an impact on all of life, including our relationships. It is John who keeps coming back to that close bond between the love of God and the love of our fellow humans. One follows from the other; if that is not the case, then one is false.

> Beloved, let us love one another, because love is from God; everyone who loves is born of God and knows God. Whoever does not love does not know God, for God is love. God's love was revealed among us in this way: God sent his only Son into the world so that we might live through him. In this is love, not that we loved God but that he loved us and sent his Son to be the atoning sacrifice for our sins. Beloved, since God loved us so much, we also ought to love one another. No one has ever seen God; if we love one another, God lives in us, and his love is perfected in us.
>
> By this we know that we abide in him and he in us, because he has given us of his Spirit. And we have seen and do testify that the Father has sent his Son as the Saviour of the world. God abides in those who confess that Jesus is the Son of God, and they abide in God. So we have known and believe the love that God has for us.
>
> God is love, and those who abide in love abide in God, and God abides in them. Love has been perfected among us in this: that we may have boldness on the day of judgment, because as he is, so are we in this world. There is no fear in love, but perfect

love casts out fear; for fear has to do with punishment, and whoever fears has not reached perfection in love. We love because he first loved us. Those who say, 'I love God', and hate their brothers or sisters, are liars; for those who do not love a brother or sister whom they have seen, cannot love God whom they have not seen. The commandment we have from him is this: those who love God must love their brothers and sisters also. (1 John 4:7-21)

In this way, our neighbour becomes God's replacement, the icon of God, the incarnation of the transcendent God. That Jesus took this identification to an extreme becomes ever clearer if we consider the conditions: "Truly I tell you, just as you did not do it to one of the least of these, you did not do it to me" (Matthew 25:45).

When we open our minds and our hearts to God's unconditional love in prayer, our lives will change. Einstein once said: "Prayer does not change the world, but prayer changes man and man the world."

Our love must be rooted in divine love if we want it to have a divine dimension. At the same time, we require support from a love called *philia*, or the love between friends. People who are not familiar with the joy of having good friends will have difficulty fulfilling the call to universal love. God's grace does not become fruitful until it finds its completion in humanity. God becomes incarnate in our lives through our talents, our personalities, our joys and our suffering. The same is true for our being in community with others: we become brothers and sisters in the full reality of our lives.

The vocation to brotherhood and sisterhood is both a divine and a human affair. The bonds that develop in a religious community form the basis for profound solidarity. Religious who are authentic are transparent; they are inviting, simple, modest, sensitive, perceptive and considerate. Others do not represent a threat to them since they engage in relationship on the basis of equality. Behind every exchange they see the individual whom they wish to respect and love. Someone becomes an enemy where there is competition, jealousy, revenge or hatred – all contrary to the bonds that unite us.

Respect and love form the basis of a new type of relationship between people. It is that new type of relationship that modern society needs and that religious can both exemplify and encourage. Anything less is undesirable.

In speaking about fraternal love, I must say something about celibacy as well. By not getting married, religious retain a certain degree of openness to everyone. This availability means that religious can have a unique understanding of relationships among humans. Their involvement stands midway between aloofness, based on the fear of giving oneself more intimately, and the desire to possess someone. Those are the two ways in which our sexuality can be expressed. Fear is not a good master, although many of us were raised in an atmosphere where sexuality remained taboo. But sexuality can become destructive when it involves our ego or the urge to satisfy one's lust. In spite of our choice to live a life of consecrated celibacy, we must not ignore our sexuality nor repress it but keep it under control. It has to be channelled through the observance of our vows, purified, and turned into a positive force. The focus of our sexuality finds its expression in asceticism and friendship. Asceticism means that we recognize and express our sexuality and that we do so consciously in our spiritual life. Love of God is why we make that sacrifice of continence. As in the case of the love of our neighbour, God's grace is indispensable. We should not try to fool ourselves. Without a profound prayer life that allows us to enter into the love of God, continence as a positive choice in life is impossible. In the absence of prayer and the love of God, continence can only be the result of a Spartan way of life that risks frustration. The search for compensations and the abuse of some circumstances to satisfy some unfulfilled desires are but two possible consequences. We are all familiar with too many religious who lack inner joy because they are burdened with deep frustrations and unfulfilled desires. However, even there, God's love continues to be an assurance that forgiveness after a moment of weakness, a lapse or a sin remains possible because love removes the sin.

Apart from asceticism, there is friendship that fulfills our deep desire for affection and tenderness. Among our friends we can be ourselves – all masks may be dropped and we no longer have to put on a show. We can reveal our joy and our grief, and we can express our affection in all honesty. Among our friends we can express our sexuality but without it becoming erotic. It is that midpoint between aloofness and the physical-erotic expression that remains underdeveloped with many religious. When it comes to touching and physical contact, some only know how to bear or to possess. There is nothing in between. The same is true for the way they look. Either they are staring into emptiness or they are spying like veritable peeping Toms. Among friends we are invited to learn to use our senses to develop relationships that bring people closer together without fear or the urge to possess. Thanks to that experience we can approach the larger community as well-balanced people who are open and accessible and who can approach others with deep respect and love.

Affirming others

When we express our love to others, we affirm them. We are saying and showing to the other that we accept them, appreciate them and wish to encourage them. Dr. Terruwe, a Dutch psychiatrist, writes, "I say that you can be you whoever you are, with your gifts and your faults, and you can become whoever you are but are as yet unable to be, and you can do so in your way and in your own tempo."[30]

Mutual affirmation contrasts sharply with self-affirmation, whereby humans do everything to get the affirmation they seek from others for themselves. We see this today in people who collect all kinds of things to make themselves interesting or to find satisfaction in life. The tragic thing, however, is that these things do not fill the void because it can never really be filled. Mutual affirmation works differently. We no longer focus on ourselves but seek to discover the good in others and affirm it. The egotistical circle around our own personality is broken and the other replaces us at the centre of it. To affirm others gives confidence, helps them grow as human beings and opens them up to others. An affirmed person, in turn, becomes an affirming person. By affirming the other we receive affirmation ourselves. A community in which mutual affirmation is cultivated is characterized by a climate of growth. People feel encouraged to develop the good that is in them. They learn to accept themselves as they are, a condition needed to learn to love oneself. Not loving others is often caused by inadequate self-love, which is in turn caused by the fact that one finds it hard to accept oneself. Mutual affirmation touches on the core of our existence – that is, self-acceptance – and gives a positive stimulus to our capacity to love.

To deal with one another in a positive way seems easy, but reality teaches us that this attitude is often thwarted by our ego and by competition. We are all inclined to feel superior and to focus on another's negative features. We develop a lot of blind spots with regard to our own behaviour. Our defence mechanisms change our standards and make us quick to discover the negative traits of others. Often we would rather talk *about* people than *to* them. Backbiting and gossip threaten community life. By speaking ill of someone, we set ourselves up as the judge of others, which is a form of self-affirmation; we affirm our qualities by comparing them with the negative characteristics of others. Like any form of self-affirmation, backbiting is a deadly tactic that poisons our relationships. That does not mean, however, that we should close our eyes to the evil done by others in order to keep the peace. On the contrary, as a sign of our love, we should have the courage to challenge others, to help them to change their attitude or to keep them from doing worse things.

A loving reprimand is not easy but is essential to bring about a profound peace for oneself and for the other. But a loving reprimand is worthy of that name only when it is the result of profound love of the other, a real concern about helping the other. When a reprimand is the result of aggression against the other because we feel angry or hurt, it will only lead to more aggression and unjustified self-defence. In that case, the reprimand is nothing more than a way of venting our emotions, and it will lead to nothing but negativism and aggression. When reprimanding in a fraternal way, we hold a mirror in front of the other, allowing the other to look himself or herself in the eye. One takes full responsibility for what the other says and uses the "I"-form. Others are given the opportunity to react, to defend themselves, and there is common ground for dialogue and for keeping emotions under control. We must avoid reprimanding others when we are emotionally hurt ourselves, because then aggression might dominate the discussion instead of love.

Mutual affirmation, as an expression of one's love, requires exercise, certainly in a community in which it is not common to talk openly about one's feelings with others. However, this is not just about feelings but about a new way of dealing with one another. It is about a new way of looking at people and of communicating this, knowing that one helps the other grow toward solidarity.

Open for forgiveness

In *Community and Growth: Our Pilgrimage Together*, Jean Vanier describes the structure of l'Arche, a community that he developed with volunteers and people with disabilities. He suggests that celebrations and forgiveness be the pillars of any community. Celebrations, as expressions of mutual love and a unique type of affirmation, are possible only when we are capable of forgiving the mistakes of others. And forgiveness is encouraged when people learn to celebrate together in love and to express their love through celebration. In a community, forgiveness is necessary since a community needs to be reformed constantly. When a group focuses on mistakes made by the members, the group will die or it will become impossible to live together. To refuse to ask for forgiveness or to grant forgiveness is the biggest sin against fraternal love. It is refusing to be a brother or sister or to accept the other as brother or sister. It is doing what Cain did when he refused to continue to consider Abel as his brother or to see himself as Abel's brother. Every time forgiveness is requested and every time forgiveness is granted, the bonds of community are restored. In other words, people become brothers and sisters again when they either grant or ask for forgiveness.

This mentality is very different from the one that characterizes modern-day society. Today, people tend to think in terms of accusation, settlement of accounts, compensation or damages, and even revenge. There is little room left for forgiveness. We find it difficult to see the difference between the bad that has been done and the person who has done it. A number of basic principles need to be considered here.

First, there is the evil as deed. It should identified as such: that is, as evil and wrong. There can be no discussion about that. But then there is the person (or persons) who have done something bad or evil. They should be capable of recognizing that they have been wrong, live with the natural consequences, but also be forgiven as soon as the wrong has been put right. There should also be the possibility to ask for mutual forgiveness without expecting punishment. There should be no link between the wrong that has been done and the punishment. Respect for the person is always more important than punishment, even when the action was extremely disrespectful. For example, in case of murder, there was no respect whatsoever for the victim. But when the murderer is punished, his life will have to be respected.

The death penalty can never be accepted because it does not respect the person, who is deprived of the chance to ask for forgiveness or be granted forgiveness or to lead a better life.

The basic principles that apply to crimes and punishments also apply to our daily dealings with one another: to label an act as good or wrong, to continue to respect the person in all circumstances, to make sure that forgiveness remains a possibility, to continue to believe in personal conversion and in the ability to take a first step towards forgiveness.

The Bible contains many examples that illustrate the importance of forgiveness. Jesus shows that he always gives the last word to forgiveness: "Neither do I condemn you. Go your way, and from now on do not sin again" (John 8:11). Even nailed to the cross, he asked, "Father, forgive them; for they do not know what they are doing" (Luke 23:34). Jesus is radical because he made his enemies subject to the commandment of love, too. Forgiveness is a consequence of love. We trust God, who is love, to do whatever we are unable to do from the emotional point of view, and we ask God to accomplish in us what we can only try to do. When a group of Trappist fathers was murdered at Tibhirine in Algeria in 1996, victims of blind extremism, we were moved by the words of the prior, Brother Christian, written some time before the tragic incident. Aware that granting forgiveness to one's enemies is difficult, he wrote about his intention to forgive in a prayer in which he asked God to grant him grace to be able to forgive.

> If it should happen one day – and it could be today –
> that I become a victim of the terrorism which now
>   seems ready to engulf
> all the foreigners living in Algeria,
> I would like my community, my church and my family
> to remember that my life was given to God and to
>   this country.

> I ask them to accept the fact
> > that the One Master of all life
> was not a stranger to this brutal departure.
> I would ask them to pray for me:
> for how could I be found worthy of such an offering?
> I ask them to associate this death with so many
> > other equally violent ones
> which are forgotten through indifference
> > or anonymity.
> My life has no more value than any other.
> Nor any less value.
> In any case, it has not the innocence of childhood.
> I have lived long enough to know that I am an
> > accomplice in the evil
> which seems to prevail so terribly in the world,
> even in the evil which might blindly strike me down.
> I should like, when the time comes, to have
> > a moment of spiritual clarity
> which would allow me to beg forgiveness of God
> and of my fellow human beings,
> and at the same time forgive with all my heart the
> > one who would strike me down.[31]

Such examples encourage us to offer forgiveness in our daily lives, in which we are faced not with life-threatening situations but rather with mundane conflicts. But our basic attitude should be the same: name the evil, ask for forgiveness or grant it, pray for our enemies, believe in the possibility of conversion and never consider something or someone as hopeless.

7

Religious Leadership

In every community there are members who are called to assume positions of leadership. Superior, prior, guardian, minister, abbot and ancillary are all titles that express something specific, and were preceded by either "mother" or "father" in the past. Today, most communities choose not to use "father" or "mother," and instead say "brother," "friar" or "sister." Thus, they wish to express the equality between the person in charge and the other members. Most importantly, religious leadership implies serving the community.

In this chapter I wish to discuss a number of features of modern-day religious leadership.

Leaders in our time

Most religious communities were founded due to the dedication and the initiative of religious leaders. Most of our founders were people who demonstrated a remarkable combination of a deeply inspired life, a strong urge to serve the community, a capacity to motivate other people, and an ability to organize all these different elements according to a very personal and specific structure. We could summarize this in four words: inspiration, service, motivation and organization.

Their inspiration started it all: a deeply evangelic life on which Jesus' message had an ever deeper and more complete impact. They let the Holy Spirit infiltrate their minds, and thus they became charismatic people who could translate the gospel in a unique way in their own environment and time. The thing that we would later describe as charism was their interpretation of life that was based on the gospel and inspired by the Spirit of God.

But their evangelical inspiration was intended to bear fruit in the world, as a service to humankind. The Word of God had to be preached, in word and in deed. The Word had to find a place to settle on this earth. They imitated Jesus – how he drew closer to humans through his preaching and through his works of charity. For everyone had to learn about the kingdom of God.

Their example of authentic evangelic life inspired others, and their first followers found inspiration in that self-same ideal. The founders understood how they could motivate their followers, and how they could let them share in their charism. The letters written by many founders illustrate how they kept trying to encourage their followers to live the radical message of the gospel.

Finally, many founders excelled at organizing. Some not only succeeded in founding a new order or new congregation, but also in creating a whole network of charitable institutions and facilities, often despite difficult circumstances, such as resistance from both ecclesiastic and civil authorities, or lack of financial means. As the organizers they had to be dynamic and inventive, but also capable of anticipating the future.

What can those four qualities of the religious leaders teach us for today? Would it be too bold a statement to say that our communities are in need of inspired leaders in service who are capable of organizing things and motivating people?

Let us examine these four qualities in the light of the current vision on leadership.

Inspiration

Today, due to a lack of personal inspiration, many management strategies do not correspond to what is expected from a manager. Companies where technicians and engineers tend to have the last word are going through a depression. They realize that success does not depend on a good market analysis, an optimized production process or well-considered financial policies. While successful companies do have well-trained technicians on staff, what is more important is that they have leaders with a vision.

More and more companies have become aware of the fact that, if they wish to become successful, they need leaders, not managers. Recent economic history has taught us that big companies, even state enterprises, that are led only by technocrats are often unsuccessful. If success depends on statistics and outcome, and if the bonds between general management, middle management and staff are broken, the company risks triggering the survival mechanisms on all levels. This means that people start leading their own lives and stop caring about meeting the company's objectives. Instead, they care more about the acquisition of personal wealth, personal power and individual benefits. If we analyze the most recent massive bankruptcies, we notice that one or several of these elements played a decisive role in the failure of the company.

Therefore, we should not be surprised that today more and more training programs are being developed and organized that focus on leadership models rather than on management skills.

Charlie Chaplin's film *Modern Times* was prophetic in that people require more than a simple analysis of their tasks. They want vision, and people to explain that vision to them. But then again we are experiencing an increasing technologization of both language and communication. Language is becoming ever more limited, more business-like. There are more than enough talk shows, but in the end nothing significant is being said in them. Thanks to e-mail and the Internet, we are capable of sending messages to the other end of the world in no time, but we have the greatest difficulty in having a normal, leisurely conversation with our neighbour. In the past, work had a double objective. It was a service to the community and allowed us to provide for ourselves. Today, many people simply work for the money. Work or labour has lost its soul. And in many cases, an important dimension of life has been lost: the dimension that refers to our innermost self, to our own existence. Human have lost their innermost selves, and have to fill the void with false securities such as power, possessions or pleasure. In some cases, people work too much, which leads to workaholism.

No matter how great his or her management skills are, no manager is capable of dealing with these problems. Only a leader who can explain a vision, stimulate involvement and give meaning to certain work can get a group to the point where it is willing to defend ideals that lie beyond the group itself, and the individuals who belong to it. That is the key to successful leadership.

This rather long discussion of the business world helps us realize that there is a parallel between worldly and spiritual leadership. Furthermore, what is socially relevant is also relevant in religious communities, for both are made up of people. However, one may expect that religious leaders let their leadership be guided by an inspiration, a vision that is fundamental. There is a risk that so-called spirituality courses give managers a kind of refuge from the totally secularized and businesslike world rather than to encourage them to reflect on the meaning of life. That would be an outright abuse of spirituality, a caricature of what true spirituality is: a methodical way of understanding reality, including its deepest dimensions. This can never result in some kind of flight from reality in order to survive. However, there is always support that helps us to face reality.

Just like the founders, religious leaders will have to be inspired people, people with a vision who can share that vision with others. They will have to be able to read the signs of the time in light of the charism of their order or congregation, and rephrase it for their brothers and sisters in an encouraging way. They will be, first of all, people who deepen their inspiration through prayer, *lectio divina*, reflection and study. They will learn about the sources from which the orders and congregations originated – the stories about the founder and the foundation – and draw from them the essential themes around which the community comes together.

To express it in more business-like terms, they will have to word the mission of the organization, experience it and live according to it. To do that, they will draw inspiration from the story about the beginning, translating it into themes for today, and developing a new professional philosophy based on it.

Helpfulness

Perhaps the most important feature of Christian leadership is that it seeks inspiration in the gospel imbued in service.

It was Jesus who introduced the idea of "servant." During the Last Supper, when Jesus washed the disciples' feet, he showed that whoever wanted to become truly great had to become a servant (see John 13:1-17). The paradox of the gospel centres on our understanding of serving others: "Whoever wishes to be great among you must be your servant" (Matthew 20:26).

This leadership through service contrasts sharply with every effort or ambition to increase power. It is not about having the last word and forcing our will upon others because we are in charge.

We do have power from a certain hierarchical position, but we get authority for what we have to say, on the basis of our inspiration and the vision that we hold.

Leadership through service aims at the well-being of the other and of the group, and not our own personal well-being. It is not about being appreciated and affirmed oneself, but about appreciating and affirming others. Leaders in service do not make decisions based on passing joys or criticism, but entirely on the well-being of others that they wish to improve. If necessary, they would sacrifice their own position to ensure that the community for which they bear responsibility attained its objectives. We remember Mikhail Gorbachev, who introduced the idea of *perestroika*, which eventually cost him his position as president.

So, leadership through service is not exclusively a Christian style of leadership. But Christian leadership should always involve a high degree of service.

Leadership that is based on Jesus' example has a double focus – on the one hand, a consciousness that we do not lead a group on the basis of our own authority, but that it is a gift and a grace from God; and on the other hand, that as leader, we are also the servant of others. Leaders modelled after Jesus are twice a servant: the servant of God and the servant of the people. The big difference between worldly leaders and leaders who feel that they have been called by God is their ultimate responsibility. Worldly leaders have projects that they wish to accomplish, relying on their own initiative, the success of which depends on their dedication, creativity, knowledge and skillfulness. They are forced to draw power from themselves, and cannot afford to give in to weakness. They must be capable of providing the right answer to whatever question is fired at them. That may lead to an unhealthy situation involving a lot of stress, because perfection is required, and perfection is difficult for humans to reach.

Religious leaders are given the task of leader because it is their calling. They are sent by God to contribute to the development of the kingdom. They believe that they are granted the power and the grace, the so-called grace of state, for which they pray. They believe that their leadership did not originate in their own inventiveness, riches or willpower, and that their leadership skills are given an extra edge through that working of grace. They realize that they are not omnipotent, and that there are questions that they cannot answer, something that they humbly admit. Their faith in God's grace gives them the assurance that no problem will remain unsolved, even though they will not always be the one who will have found the solution. Their personal involvement is linked to their confidence that the right solution will eventually be found. Impatience and resistance are signs of a lack of faith and trust in God's grace.

The basic attitude of the servant-leader is humility. That double focus encourages us to adopt a humble attitude: a great dependence on God, our Creator, and the fact that we are called and sent to serve humankind. Humility does not discourage us: rather, it gives us courage! We do not have to solve everything ourselves, but we may live in and with the grace of God. Humility also finds positive power in humour based on the idea that there is no need for us to be perfect. When we make mistakes, we acknowledge them and laugh about them, as long as we honestly try to do good and to serve the truth. Finally, it is humility that offers the remedy against nervous exhaustion, the result of an exaggerated sense of responsibility. We do what we have to do seriously but with a seriousness that is somewhat playful.

Cardinal Danneels listed five qualities that may help us to evaluate our Christian leadership.[32]

First and foremost, leadership involves a great sense of responsibility that, in the right doses, should not cause leaders to suffer nervous exhaustion or to become scrupulous or indifferent. However, since they are aware that they are carried by God, they feel ready to consciously assume their own responsibility or even to take the risk of transferring a certain amount of responsibility. There are no frenetic efforts.

A second quality is accessibility. Leaders should leave room for spontaneous meetings, an unprepared discussion, and quick anticipation of a situation.

Third, servant-leaders have to continue giving the highest priority to the poor and the weak. That means that, when taking decisions, they will have to allow themselves to be led by the principle of human dignity, and make sure that everyone's dignity is respected, and even improved.

Fourth, when others fail to fulfill their task or mission, Christian leaders must be able to follow the example of a God who gives orders, provides strength and grants forgiveness. It is a heavy duty, an ideal that is hard to attain, but at the same time a triad that characterizes Christian leadership.

Finally, Christian leaders should pay attention to the values that were mentioned in the Sermon on the Mount, such as poverty, patience, gentleness, purity and peacefulness (Matthew 5:1-12). They are the fruits of the Holy Spirit that Paul mentions in his letter to the Galatians: love, joy, peace, patience, kindness, generosity, faithfulness, gentleness, and self-control (Galatians 5). Those qualities, in addition to a healthy dose of creativity, courage and endurance, make a competent Christian servant-leader.

The poet Adriaan Roland Holst (1888–1976) described that "being at the people's service" most strikingly:

> I do not demand a harvest, for I have no barns,
> I am at your servant without having any possessions...
> I will never again see the haulms, neither shall I ever
> bind them into sheaves again, but make me believe
> in the harvest for which you put me into service ...

Organizing

Religious leaders need good organizational skills, drawing on their own inspiration about service. Organization involves matching people with tasks and structuring them in a way that common goals can be reached. Religious communities are based on several principles that are at the same time solid and pertinent.

- Religious communities hold a principle of democracy whereby members, through representation in the chapter, elect their own leaders for a certain period.
- Administration is collegial and allows for open policies. All leaders are supported by a council with whom they share responsibility. Leaders do not function in isolation, and there are healthy restrictions on a leader's powers.
- Religious communities hold the principle of subsidiarity whereby a higher body refrains from acting or taking decisions if a lower body is qualified to do it. This encourages leaders at all levels to assume full responsibility.
- Actions are taken on the basis of a clear policy. There is the charism that is formulated and concretized in the Rule or the constitutions that are regularly updated during the chapters, the result of which are the directories. A chapter is always an important event for a religious order or congregation because, apart from the evaluation of the past period, a policy for the future is written. Finally, it is remarkable how the organization of a religious community is always embedded in the environment and never isolated (even though people claim that sometimes). Since orders and congregations are part of the church, the church participates, giving direction, formulating invitations and giving stimuli. Because of the pastoral motivation, there is also a strong link with society that continues to challenge and question the church. International groups are confronted with a considerable multicultural input that plays an increasingly prominent role because of the shifts that take place in orders and congregations.

On the more personal level, we may expect religious leaders to possess certain organizational qualities. In a separate paragraph I will discuss a number of features listed in the Rule of Benedict, and the current vision of servant-leadership.

Motivating

Finally, we may expect religious leaders to be capable of motivating and encouraging their fellow brothers and sisters so that they may give the best of themselves. The image of the prophet who does not despair but keeps the vision alive, encouraging others to live according to that vision, thereby making it come true, is used quite often in this respect.

No one is born a prophet, and no one can call themselves a prophet. It is a charism that one is granted, to which one is called, and for which reason one is sent into the world.

Every community needs a few prophets who translate the story of the past into a vision for the future. We may believe that God sends these prophets to the communities. But the community is sometimes both deaf and blind to the words and the presence of its prophets. The vision that no one is recognized as a prophet in his or her own country continues to be repeated, even today. People are still killing prophets today or silencing them because they tend to criticize or disturb an easy and privileged existence.

Communities that do not kill their prophets or silence them but rather that listen to them and follow their instructions show that they are willing to think about and live in the future. They do not want to linger in the past, but look to what the future will bring, seeking new perspectives. In addition to the so-called prophetic leaders, we also need missionary leaders who regard it as their mission to put into practice the prophetic message in and with their community. Some prophets are impatient or unstable, which makes it difficult for them to set off with a group of "fast ones" and "slow ones," "followers" and "skeptics" or even "troublemakers."

We need missionary leaders who succeed in making the prophet's words acceptable, presenting them as a challenge. Missionary leaders are able to motivate people to take their contribution seriously, even if that contribution is but a small part of a larger whole. Those building the cathedrals did just that: their meticulous but hard work was considered as part of a project that transcended even individual life. They were called to believe in the harvest; that was enough.

From time to time people need to be encouraged and affirmed so that their task, small and insignificant though it may seem, contributes to the realization of the overall mission of the order or congregation. In this respect, it would be wrong to forget or ignore the elderly and sick religious who, in a non-active way, but no less intensely, continue to support the group's project through their interest, their prayer and, in a very mystical way, their suffering.

Today's religious leaders must possess a combination of these four qualities – inspiration, service, motivation and organization – since they are the pillars of every Christian servant-leadership. I will now test this vision of servant-leadership against the image of leader in one of the oldest monastic rules, the Benedictines.

Benedictine leadership

A symbol of the Benedictine leadership could be the stethoscope: listening attentively to what is alive in the other. The 64th chapter of the centuries-old rule of Benedict treats of the role of the abbot. The following quotes help us to understand Benedictine leadership.

> In the election of an Abbot let this always be observed as a rule, that he be placed in the position whom the whole community with one consent, in the fear of God, or even a small part, with sounder judgement, shall elect. But let him who is to be elected be chosen for the merit of his life and the wisdom of his doctrine, though he be the last in the community.
>
> But even if the whole community should by mutual consent elect a man who agreeth to connive at their evil ways (which God forbid) and these irregularities in some come to the knowledge of the Bishop to

whose diocese the place belongeth, or to neighbouring Abbots, or Christian people, let them not permit the intrigue of the wicked to succeed, but let them appoint a worthy steward over the house of God, knowing that they shall receive a bountiful reward for this action, if they do it with a pure intention and godly zeal; whereas, on the other hand, they commit a sin if they neglect it.

But when the Abbot hath been elected let him bear in mind how great a burden he hath taken upon himself, and to whom he must give an account of his stewardship (Luke 16:2); and let him be convinced that it becometh him better to serve than to rule. He must, therefore, be versed in the divine law, that he may know whence "to bring forth new things and old" (Matthew 13:52). Let him be chaste, sober, and merciful, and let him always exalt "mercy above judgement" (James 2:13), that he also may obtain mercy.

Let him hate vice, but love the brethren. And even in his corrections, let him act with prudence and not go to extremes, lest, while he aimeth to remove the rust too thoroughly, the vessel be broken. Let him always keep his own frailty in mind, and remember that "the bruised reed must not be broken" (Isaiah 42:3). In this we are not saying that he should allow evils to take root, but that he cut them off with prudence and charity, as he shall see it is best for each one, as we have already said; and let him aim to be loved rather than feared.

Let him not be fussy or over-anxious, exacting or headstrong; let him not be jealous or suspicious, because he will never have rest. In all his commands, whether they refer to things spiritual or temporal, let him be cautious and considerate. Let him be discerning and temperate in the tasks which he enjoineth, recalling the discretion of holy Jacob who saith: "If I should cause my flocks to be overdriven, they would all die in one day" (Genesis 33:13). Keeping in view these and other dictates of discretion, the mother of virtues, let him so temper everything that the strong may still have something to desire and the weak may not draw back. Above all, let him take heed that he keep this Rule in all its detail; that when he hath served well he may hear from the Lord what the good servant heard who gave his fellow-servants bread in season: "Amen, I say to you," He saith, "he shall set him over all his goods" (Matthew 24:47).[33]

In his book *A Rule of Life for Beginners*, Wil Deckse discusses these passages and gives them a practical application for a community of friars.[34]

1 – The abbot must always bear in mind how the other friars address him.

He is the abba or father. He should act like a loving father and relate to the friars as a father relates to his children. He should be concerned about them, encourage their development and growth, trust them, and let go of them when necessary. A father who prevents his son or daughter from reaching adulthood, who continues to consider them as children incapable of defending themselves, is not a good father. True fatherly love implies being able to lovingly let go of your children, trusting them to find their own way in life. Remember the father who let his prodigal son go, giving him his freedom, but waiting for him with open arms when he decided to return home again.

2 – Let the abbot bear in mind that he has accepted the difficult and trying task of guiding his friars' souls. And let him be convinced that it is more becoming to serve than to rule.

He has the task of leading souls, that is, motivating people, orienting them and encouraging them to take action.

It is a demanding task because he is dealing with people with different backgrounds, ambitions and needs. Some people claim that there is no greater injustice than equality. No two humans on earth are identical. Benedict continues: "He should approach one generously, and gently; another, he should reprimand, and still another, he should try to convince."[35] The essence is that he should do everything in a true spirit of service. The leader is the servant. The one who is in charge should be capable of listening attentively to the condition of his friars' souls, and respond appropriately to each friar's soul. I return to the image of a doctor using a stethoscope to listen quietly and attentively before making a diagnosis or suggesting a particular kind of therapy. How often do we quickly start with the therapy without having listened attentively, in order to make a good diagnosis.

3 – The abbot will adapt his approach according to everyone's nature, and everyone's comprehension. He will, in fact, yield to them.

We are not used to hearing that a leader should give in to his subject's nature. The word flexibility is important here. If he really wants people to grow, then the leader should sympathize with others, imagine himself in the other's position in order to give direction and to encourage them to grow and to blossom. A golden rule for the leader is that he should show interest in the other's life and not remain business-like, sticking to the order of the day. People ought to feel and hear that they are known by their leader and appreciated; then they can grow and flourish.

4 – And, of course, there is the abbot's own soul.

Some leaders tend to forget to care for their own souls. They must remain in touch with sources and values that can guide them. But, in practice, often the more souls a leader has to guide, the more he neglects his own soul. The leader has no time to read a spiritual book, to walk in nature, to play sports, to get together with friends.

A lot depends on how well leaders manage their time. They need to establish a good flow to their day according to the following four skills, inspired by the Benedictine methodology:

• The art of starting: Do they start the day with essential items that were planned or do they let unexpected needs, such as incoming mail or unannounced visitors, shape their day? Some people are busy all day without actually doing what they need to do.

• The art of stopping: When the bell rings, the Benedictines stop what they are doing, even if they have not quite finished their work. This prevents them from continuing until they are exhausted, and encourages them to live in the present. When we stop doing one thing with a good attitude, then we can start something else with a good attitude. The art of starting and the art of stopping are linked.

• The art of adopting the right attitude between the starting and the stopping: As we are working on something, we often fret about the past or worry about something that is still to come. This has a very negative impact on the quality of our work. Have you noticed how poorly a conversation proceeds if one of the persons involved cannot stop referring to the past or is already thinking about their next conversation partner? Often, at receptions, some people tend to glance around, trying to locate their next conversation partner.

Trying to live in the present is a good remedy against nervous exhaustion: We can become exhausted if we are surprised by a series of tasks that prevent us from doing one task at a time. Start with one task, finish it, and then start the second. At the end of the day you will be surprised by how much you have accomplished. The working rhythm becomes calmer, and in the end you accomplish more. Even if your agenda is full, you can do your job in a relaxed and dignified way every day.

• The art of respecting the rhythms of the day: We need to remember the morning rituals, accept the day happily and hopefully as a gift from God, the moments of peace during which we reflect, and the evening rituals during which we evaluate the day, and let go of our work. Through reflection we can establish an order to the day, planning how best to use our energy from morning until evening.

As to leaders' personal well-being, it is important to have a group of friends with whom they can be themselves, and talk freely about whatever they like. Cornelis Verhoeven calls this "the safe zone." In that group others should be able to say what is on their minds about you as leader. Leaders must realize that a lot of things remain unsaid because people are afraid to say them, or that people approve of certain behaviours because their position does not permit them to speak their minds openly. Thus leaders may end up in a kind of dream world, thinking it reality. As soon as they have to give up or lose their position as leaders, they grow disillusioned because people whom they thought to be friends do not appear to be their friends at all, making them feel abandoned and betrayed by everyone. Leaders need *correctio fraterna* whereby their subordinates can make remarks on their attitudes, opinions, policies, etc.

5 – An abbot must be chaste, moderate and charitable.

Here the stress is on the leader's function as example. People accept the leadership of those who mean what they say, who live what they preach. Authenticity is of the essence.

6 – An abbot should not be hasty, fearful, stubborn, jealous or suspicious, "or otherwise he will never find peace." Personal unrest is contagious and can eventually damage the entire community. Haste is synonymous with making mistakes, fear leads to constraint, stubbornness inhibits flexibility, jealousy makes the organization go sour, and suspicion leads to reactions that confirm and reinforce existing suspicions. I remember a superior from my time as a student who was always on the lookout to check if we came home on time in the evenings. After a few weeks almost

everyone had a key to the back door so that we could get in and out whenever we wanted.

Peacefulness encourages meticulous work; gladness inspires us with confidence, and takes away our fear and the fear of others; openness to other solutions than our own is conducive to the decision-making process; taking pleasure in other people's good performances, and expressing that, and affirming that, may stimulate the others to perform even better; and a basic attitude of trust inclines one to be really open to the other.

7 – Let the abbot hate evil, but love the brothers.

Naturally, that is a golden rule that ought to be used, when we – as leader – have to adjust the conduct or attitude of others. We should not avoid the situation, but have the courage to talk about something that is going wrong. However, we should always do this out of love, and with love for our fellow brother. Whenever we make a remark out of aggression, we can expect aggression in return. Aggression generates aggression. It is important in this respect to be able to turn a page, to say that, and to do it. "Go, and do not sin anymore!"

8 – Let the abbot arrange everything with such a feeling of measure so that there is still something to expect for the strong, and that the weak are not frightened.

Benedictine leadership is clearly a matter of knowing where to draw the line. Leaders should not want to be part of everything since that can stifle others. They should not try to do everything themselves because they think that the others can't contribute. They should take care that the others are given every opportunity to contribute, and that the weak are encouraged to what is possible.

Leaders devote a lot of attention to the weak, to problems and to grumblers. This attention is necessary. But also the so-called strong, those who seem capable of taking care of themselves, need attention and affirmation, too. Leaders should make sure that everyone is doing well, that the community sets off from the vision that the members developed together. Anselm Grün puts it like this: "Leading means first of all bringing people to life, stimulating the life inside them. Leading is the art of finding the key to the treasure of one's staff."[36]

Leadership in service

The 20th century was characterized by a range of management theories that focused on management through control and implementation. "Planning," "motivating," "controlling" and "evaluating" were words that were often used. Even the formulation of a mission statement was influenced by that approach. It was a way to meet the objectives through a stronger, more streamlined corps d'esprit.

All these elements are valuable, but say very little about the leader. Today, more and more people are convinced that success depends on a leader's personality, and on the way in which they identify themselves with the cause. It reminds me of former French President Charles de Gaulle, who would end every speech with the rather pathetic expression "La France, c'est moi!" He had identified himself completely with his country.

A vision that is becoming ever more popular is outlined in Robert K. Greenleaf's book *The Servant as Leader*. In his introduction, Greenleaf explains the origins of this concept.

> I got the idea of the servant as leader reading Journey to the East by Herman Hesse. It is a story about a group of people on a journey. The key character in the story, Leo, is the group's servant who takes care of the household chores; he also gives the group courage through his spiritual powers and his singing. He has an extraordinary personality. Everything goes well until the day Leo disappears. Almost immediately, the group starts falling apart, and eventually they decide to cancel the rest of the journey.

Everyone feels the same: "It is no use to go on without Leo." The storyteller, a member of the group, continues to travel for several years and eventually finds Leo. The storyteller joins the Order that had initiated the original journey. There he discovers that Leo, whom he had known as a servant, was in fact the head of the Order, an inspiring guide, a great and noble leader.[37]

Greenleaf concluded that all great leaders initially should be servants. True leadership develops naturally in people who are motivated to help others, and whose vision and mission are based on service.

Servant-leadership is a new type of leadership. The essential characteristics of servant-leadership are being at the service of others and creating a positive environment for everyone. It is a spiritual approach to leadership that embraces trust, unity and shared responsibility, and a shared decision-making approach.

According to Greenleaf, the best way to evaluate if we are developing that type of leadership is to ask: "Are the ones whom I serve growing as persons? Are they becoming healthier, wiser, more free, more independent? Are they developing, wanting to become servants themselves?"

In his work, Greenleaf describes ten characteristics of servant-leaders. I list them below and then examine how we implement these traits.

1) Listening: Leaders demonstrate their qualities in the way they communicate and in their capacity to make good decisions. These qualities give servant-leaders power and meaning because they allow leaders to listen attentively to others, and the others feel that the leader understands what they are thinking. It is putting themselves second, being a real servant. By opening up they empathize with the other person's story. Gordon's "active listening" is important in this respect.

2) Empathizing: This is a logical outcome to listening actively: leaders try to understand the other person in an empathic way. People need to feel accepted and recognized in their specific and unique personality.

3) Making whole: Restoring and repairing relationships with others are powerful tools for transformation and integration. Many people have been hurt and are out of balance. That is part of our human condition. Servant-leaders recognize the opportunity to help others restore harmony within themselves. Greenleaf says, "Something very subtle is transmitted to someone who is led and served, when he or she realizes that the search for 'wholeness' is a mutual aspiration of both the leader and the one who is being led."[38]

4) Awareness: Awareness in general and self-awareness in particular make a strong leader. It can be frightening to choose to be aware: we never know what we will discover! Consciousness helps us to understand certain dimensions to our values and choices. We are able to study most situations in their totality. Greenleaf remarks, "Consciousness does not guarantee ease or encouragement, rather the opposite. It disturbs peacefulness, and wakes one up. Good leaders are mostly people who are 'razor-sharp' and who are reasonably worried. They do not seek to feel comfortable. They can rely on their own inner peace."[39]

5) Convincing: Servant-leaders rely on "explanation and the power of their convictions" instead of relying on their positions. They seek dialogue so that everyone gets the opportunity to present their point of view or discuss their feelings, rather than choosing to debate where often there is only one winner and many losers. They do not try to force others to comply, but convince them with their vision and arguments. They inspire and motivate others by their own enthusiasm. That is one of the most significant differences between the traditional authoritarian model and servant-leaders. A servant-leader knows that consensus and

commitment are basic conditions for implementing vision and mission.

6) Conceptualizing: Servant-leaders are characterized by their capacity "to dream big dreams" and to develop visions. They think beyond everyday reality. They can share their spirituality with others, and thus can develop their vision. In a rather contagious way, they enthuse others for their mission. For many leaders, that quality requires discipline and a lot of practice. Traditional managers are focused on attaining operational, short-term objectives. Leaders who want to become servant-leaders need to broaden their minds to conceptual thinking, which allows them to make different kinds of decisions. Servant-leaders are called to seek a balance between conceptual thinking and a reality-based approach. Achieving that balance makes them, in turn, highly efficient.

7) Foresight: Foresight implies seeing the possible consequences of a certain situation, a skill that is very much related to that of conceptualizing. It is hard to define but easily recognizable: seeing gives us knowledge. Foresight helps servant-leaders understand lessons from the past, the reality of the present, and the possible consequences of a decision for the future. Foresight is deeply rooted in intuition. Some are born with it, others develop it. In the world of leadership, it is unexplored territory. Using foresight, entrepreneurs are able to anticipate new trends, and respond to them.

8) Stewardship or "managing" instead of "owning": Peter Block, author of *Stewardship* and *The Empowered Manager*, defines stewardship as "holding something in trust for another." Greenleaf looks at organizations in this way: "Direction, management, staff and co-workers each play an essential role to safeguard their organization to the benefit of the greater good of society as a whole. Just like stewardship, the point of departure for leadership in service are the needs of the others. The stress is not on control, but on openness and conviction."[40]

9) Dedication to the growth of people: Servant-leaders believe in the intrinsic value of people that goes beyond the concrete work that they do. That is why servant-leaders are involved in and are responsible for the personal, spiritual and professional growth of every individual in the organization. In practice, that might imply making means and facilities available, showing personal interest for everyone's ideas and suggestions, fostering the involvement of co-workers in the decision-making processes and, last but not least, actively helping find a new perspective for someone who is having difficulties.

10) Building a community: Servant-leaders are aware that a lot has been lost in recent history. Human life is no longer determined by small communities but by large institutions. This awareness encourages the servant-leader to become actively involved in the formation of real communities, and an increased solidarity among people who live and work within a certain organization. This dedication does promote community building in society. Greenleaf says, "What we need to build these communities, as viable forms of life for large quantities of people, once again, is a sufficient number of leaders in service who guide us, not towards large-scale actions, but to showing the unlimited liability for a specific community."[41]

Greenleaf's vision is precious to us because it is completely in line with the preceding one, where we also stressed the importance of being a servant.

8

Moved by Charity

Our vocation to live a consecrated life, and our respect for our religious vows, can be seen as a mission. We are called to walk in Jesus' footsteps: "He has sent me to bring good news to the oppressed, to bind up the brokenhearted, to proclaim liberty to the captives, and release to the prisoners; to proclaim the year of the Lord's favour, and the day of vengeance of our God; to comfort all who mourn" (Isaiah 61:1-2). Passion for God brings about a passion for all humans without exception, and especially for those who, as both Isaiah and Jesus say, are yet to be saved.

Religious can be seen as a form of yeast. Even though we are a small minority in the church (0.12% of all the church, of which 72.5% are female religious, and 27.5% male religious) – modest and humble in number – we are nevertheless called to be signs of new life. In *Vita Consecrata*, religious life is described as "a particularly clear indication of the heavenly kingdom for the church and the world. It bundles a diversity of ways of life, spiritual traditions, and apostolic works that bear witness to the multiform grace of Christ, the presence of the Spirit, and the power of the gospel" (*VC*, 5).

Johann Baptist Metz identifies two essential functions of consecrated life: to inspire the church and to critique or correct the church.[42] When the church is facing new questions and challenges, religious can recognize the concerns and respond creatively. That is where religious play a renewing and inspiring role.

It is also the task of religious to remind the church of its real mission when it "runs the risk of losing its original fervour, and of neutralizing its own identity through all sorts of compromises."[43] As critics and correctors, to put it somewhat figuratively, we shake the tree every now and then. Will we continue to fill that role?

I now will reflect on our vows to see how they encourage a passion for humankind. To use Metz's words: How does the mystical passion for God become a political passion for humans? One passion flows from another. I then will describe a number of areas in which religious must be present. Finally, I will deal with the question of how compassion can become mercy.

Prophetic dimensions

Our vows find their origin and purpose in the mysticism of imitation, and aim to create a space in our hearts for God's passion for us and our passion for God. Our vows have an impact on the way we deal with ourselves, our neighbours and the world around us.

By observing the vow of chastity in a non-marital state in life, religious live in solidarity with all those who did not choose to remain single and who experience that loneliness as a heavy burden. These people are no longer the exception if we consider the statistics. One out of three Belgians lives alone, in many cases as the result of a break-up with their partner. Often these people suffer from isolation, and from an existential aloneness of not having someone to come home to. Also, people with a disability or an incurable illness often find their lives painful due to the fact that they may never have a family of their own.

People who live alone can find consolation and courage in meeting people who freely choose to remain unmarried, and who show that they live a well-balanced and satisfying life. Religious, by their life-state, also demonstrate that existential aloneness is a fundamental part of being human, since all human beings remain alone in the depths of themselves. Even the most intense human relationship cannot fill our deepest emptiness: only God, who waits for us in the hereafter, can do this. This reality is seldom discussed these days, so many consider this existential emptiness as pathological, as a consequence of an unsatisfying human relationship, or they may constantly seek to fill that emptiness. Because of their way of life, religious are living proof that the non-marital state in life does not necessarily lead to solitude or frustration.

The vow of chastity is also symbolic in this world where so much attention is given to sexuality and eroticism, which in most cases is an isolated sexuality, an eroticism that is separate from the most intimate type of relationship that exists between people. Often sexuality is objectified in the form of pornography, which separates people from their human dignity. Or its significance is reduced to something purely erotic, implying that no relationship is possible without some kind of sexual relating. By making the vow of chastity, religious show that a life of continence does not have to be frustrating, that interpersonal relationships can be intense without involving a sexual dimension.

Finally, a consequence of the unmarried state in life is that people are really free and available. The greater availability of religious opens the way for involvement, a degree of mobility that cannot be expected from others for practical reasons. Their willingness to venture into dengerous locations or to stay there despite the danger, and their commitment to people who no longer count in society, create unique opportunities for religious to experience the gospel message of love on the margins.

When religious become frustrated because of a sexual continence that they have not dealt with, crave the thing that they are denied, become narrow-minded or withdraw to a spiritualized world instead of being available, they become caricatures and a negative witness to religious life.

It is up to us to examine ourselves constantly: are we spiritualizing our vow? Is it still fruitful? Chittister writes,

> The function of celibacy is not to be loveless; the function of celibacy is to love without limitation, to lay down my life in loving commitment to more than those who love me. The celibate can afford to be courageous. The celibate can afford to be rejected. A wounded and abandoned world needs religious lovers who love everyone with the heart full of Divine madness. The forgotten of the world need religious who live their humanity, like them in everything but despair and dedicated to bringing hope, bringing help so that life tomorrow can be better than life today in the name of the One who came "that they may have life and have it more abundantly."[44]

Metz gives the following description of the vow of chastity:

> The evangelical virtue of remaining unmarried in fact consists in impatiently and ardently expecting the Day of the Lord. It is a type of expectance that does not tolerate any form of compromise, and that does not shun the appeal of solitude. It has to do with being radically gripped by the coming Rule of God, and with serving that coming with full commitment. Thus, it drives those who chose to remain unmarried, as imitation, to the lonely, and to those who have become isolated, and to those who are numbly caught in a life void of expectations.[45]

In *Vita Consecrata,* the prophetic mission of consecrated chastity is regarded as a challenge, given the dominantly hedonistic culture in society: "The reply of the consecrated life is above all in the joyful living of perfect chastity, as a witness to the power of God's love manifested in the weakness of the human condition" (*VC*, 88).

The vow of obedience calls religious to be attentive to the world, and to allow themselves to be touched and moved by the suffering in the world. It is imitating Christ who patiently and compassionately stood by the side of the afflicted, and who was prepared to do whatever it took to heal people's hurts. Obedience, in other words, implies carrying on the work of healing started by Jesus. It is going with God to where the people cry, and to cry with God about the deep suffering. We read in Exodus: "Then the Lord said, 'I have observed the misery of my people who are in Egypt; I have heard their cry on account of their taskmasters. Indeed, I know their sufferings'" (Exodus 3:7). The whole process of deliverance must be seen in the context of God's compassion for humankind. God sent his son to set us free. Obedience means walking in Jesus' footsteps and following him, not according to our own plans, but like he did: standing alongside people, healing, curing and reconciling them.

It also brings us closer to those who are oppressed and silenced. Metz writes, "Obedience as evangelical virtue is a radical, uncalculated devotion of life to God, the Father, who edifies and delivers man. It encourages the obedient to be close to those according to whom obedience is anything but a virtue, but rather is a sign of oppression, paternalism, and proof of the incapacity to defend oneself."[46]

Consecrated obedience becomes prophetic, taking on a political dimension, when it motivates people to stand in solidarity with all who suffer and are oppressed, and when it generates a concrete commitment to address the situation that causes suffering or oppression.

In *Vita Consecrata,* the vow of obedience is linked to the experience of freedom. "Indeed, the Son's attitude discloses the mystery of human freedom as the path of obedience to the Father's will, and the mystery of obedience as the path to the gradual conquest of true freedom" (*VC*, 91). It is an experience of freedom that differs from society's stance of emancipation and independence, with freedom of action and thinking. The vow of obedience invites us to place our freedom within the frame of reference that leads to what is good, beautiful and true, and that helps humans to develop all aspects of themselves. Going beyond the superficial is reflected in the evolution of the field of law where absolute self-determination is expected. Thus, humans limit themselves instead of becoming free. Respect for life precedes self-determination.

Metz writes that experiencing the vow of poverty "as evangelical virtue is a form of protest against the dictatorship of property, of ownership, and of pure self-affirmation. It drives those who observe the vow of poverty to a practical form of solidarity with the poor, to whom poverty is all but a virtue, but their life situation and a social reality."[47] As with the two other vows, Metz establishes a connection between the vow of poverty and solidarity with the poor. It is about the way in which we deal with goods, ranging from the use of our own goods to the exploitation of the riches of the earth. Poverty invites us to use the riches of the earth in order to further develop the world and to promote humanity in the world. A frugal lifestyle invites religious to share what they have in life. They must be able to say, "I've had enough," and they must combine that attitude with the ability to share what they have.

The vow is also an invitation to become closer to those who are poor. It is the most concrete form of solidarity that we can have. It also implies taking the side of the poor, becoming their brother or sister, and even their friend. A bishop once said, "A religious should have a number of poor people among his best friends." That prevents us from becoming paternalistic, from feeling superior, and from making others feel indebted to us.

The example of Vincent de Paul can help us. He promoted the poor to the rank of Lord and Master as a way of countering that negative trend of paternalism. He saw the poor as the icons of Christ, and considered service to the poor equally important to religion. It is striking that Vincent's attitude is described explicitly in *Vita Consecrata*, making a clear link between the passion of and for God and the passion for the poor:

> The quest for divine beauty impels consecrated persons to care for the deformed image of God on the faces of their brothers and sisters, faces disfigured by hunger, faces disillusioned by political promises, faces humiliated by seeing their culture despised, faces frightened by constant and indiscriminate violence, the anguished faces of minors, the hurt and humiliated faces of women, the tired faces of migrants who are not given a warm welcome, the faces of the elderly who are without even the minimum conditions for a dignified life. (*VC*, 75)

In *Vita Consecrata,* the vow of poverty is described as follows: "Another challenge today is that of a materialism which craves possessions, heedless of the needs and sufferings of the weakest, and lacking any concern for the balance of natural resources" (*VC*, 89).

Where religious must be present

Based in the prophetic role, through the observance of our vows, we can start to identify the places where religious are to be active. Joan Chittister writes: "What is needed now is a model of political compassion, universalism, an ecology of life, justice and peace if the planet is to survive and all its people are to live decent human lives." She adds, "What religious life needs now is the cultivation of virtues, of spiritual disciplines that enable religious to respond to these new issues with personal strength, contemplative consciousness, and common focus. There is an obvious tendency to seek refuge in internal activities that foster religious perfection. However, when the gospel, to which we claim to devote our lives, should be a reality in our lives, our religious commitment should aim radically at others."[48]

We must be careful not to withdraw to the safety of the convent. In this time of aging religious, there is a tendency to withdraw from active life. Religious life is suffering from a certain fatigue, a tendency to put everything in the past tense. We need to struggle against that tendency to withdraw from the world. This attitude goes against the gospel. When we claim to be apostolic, we need to be one hundred percent apostolic!

A second invitation is the need to develop a proper strategy for religious to be able to deal with the larger challenges of today. This strategy must be grounded in personal strength, in contemplative consciousness and in shared commitment. It is important to reflect on these three components. We may expect personal commitment from individual religious. They are called to be prophets through radical observance of their vows. Their passion for God must turn into a passion for all humans. Personal strength will always be a consequence of a contemplative conscience. It implies facing reality with the power and the mercy of God, but also with God's eyes and ears. Religious always belong to a community that supports them and gives them inspiration to see reality from a pastoral perspective. The charism of the community is a source of inspiration. God's Spirit remains active in and through the religious community, whose members bear the fruit and share it.

It is from this basic attitude that we deal with reality: with an open mind, and actively entering into the questions that are asked of us. Our answers, according to Chittister, will have to be marked by political mercy, universalism, ecology, justice and peace. We are still dealing with a passion for humanity that is translated concretely in several areas. Based on recent documents and studies on religious life, I distinguish three main areas: the deification and dehumanization of humans, divine obfuscation, and the world. (This distinction is in fact artificial, since everything is centred on the human person.)

Deified and dehumanized humans

Jan Koenot identified these two tendencies in his analysis of contemporary culture: "On the one hand man is deified, but he is dehumanized on the other."[49] His words echo the call not to consider humans as idols, and not to treat them as monsters. Humans who feel threatened in different phases and situations of their lives must be respected and affirmed in their full dignity.

Religious must focus on life, and on how to defend it from beginning to end. We will need to be present in the world of education. We need to be beside people who are sick, aged and have disabilities, and care for them. Based in justice and solidarity, we try to help and support the poor, both structurally and practically. We must be attentive to today's needy and outcast: refugees, homeless people and addicts. Let's explore each of these in a little more depth.

- *Defending life from the beginning until the end.* Based on a misinterpretation of emancipation and self-determination, the community tends to ignore the link between the beginning and the end of life and the universal and absolute idea of respect for life. Those who are weakest are deprived of protection, a flagrant violation of their integrity as human persons. Religious, thanks to our passion for humans, will be particularly sensitive to this evolution, and we will do whatever we can to protect any life that is threatened.
- *The world of education.* Throughout history, the church, represented by religious, has always placed importance on the formation and education of young people in order to teach them Christian values and to prepare them for a Christian life.

In *Vita Consecrata* we find a double mission for religious who are active in the field of education:

> Consecrated persons are able to be especially effective in educational activities and to offer a specific contribution to the work of other educators. Equipped with this charism, consecrated persons

can give life to educational undertakings permeated by the Gospel spirit of freedom and charity, in which young people are helped to mature humanly under the action of the Spirit ... The preferential love for the poor finds a special application in the choice of means capable of freeing people from that grave form of poverty which is the lack of cultural and religious training. (VC, 96, 97)

• *The care of the sick, the elderly and people with a disability*. Vita Consecrata is very clear on this point:

In the footsteps of the Divine Samaritan, physician of souls and bodies, and following the example of their respective founders and foundresses, those consecrated persons committed to this ministry by the charism of their Institute should persevere in their witness of love towards the sick, devoting themselves to them with profound understanding and compassion. They should give a special place in their ministry to the poorest and most abandoned of the sick, such as the elderly, and those who are handicapped, marginalized or terminally ill, and to the victims of drug abuse and the new contagious diseases. (VC, 83)

At the same time, religious are called to take care that the places where health care is organized remain places where gospel values are fully respected, and where people are trained to carry out these values.

• *A preferential love for the poor based on principles such as justice and solidarity*. Jesus was inspired by a preferential love for the poor and the sick. By imitating Jesus, we do the same. So many people live below the poverty level, are marginalized, and consequently no longer count in society. Justice demands that we respect them and work to improve their human dignity. Whatever help we offer must always aim at putting an end to all situations of oppression. Every form of discrimination or marginalization must be challenged. Paul says, "There is no longer Jew or Greek, there is no longer slave or free, there is no longer male and female; for all of you are one in Christ Jesus. And if you belong to Christ, then you are Abraham's offspring, heirs according to the promise" (Galatians 3:28-29). In a culture of true compassion we must build alternative experiences in which the poor and the weak can be integrated. It is also essential that these alternatives influence the broader society in a positive way. Solidarity calls us to share with those who have less, and to create systems where solidarity can develop into institutionalized and broadly accepted social systems. A purely personal solidarity must include our hope for a more structured type of solidarity.

• *Special attention for the new needy*. With every era, new groups of poor people emerge who need our compassion and solidarity. Because of our greater availability, a consequence of our vows, we will be among the first who approach these people, thus giving a sign to the world that they deserve our attention. Today's needy include refugees, homeless people, street children and addicts who cannot find a place in existing treatment facilities. It is inspiring to see how many religious are committed to these groups throughout the world.

Divine obfuscation

A second area in which religious can play an important role is helping people discover God. We live in an era of godlessness. A new spiritual movement has emerged whereby people create their own religion. On certain continents, sects have become a real plague. All sorts of demagogues succeed in attracting people's attention. All this has obscured the belief in a personal God. Professionally, religious are God-seekers, and through their entire being they demonstrate that God can indeed fulfill one's life completely. Their testimony and example can encourage people to once again ask questions about God. To do that, religious must bear witness to their passion of and for God, and show that they as a community are willing to share their prayers with others. Religious communities can also play an important role in the area of ecumenism.

In the world

Religious need to be attentive to trends and evolutions in the world.

- *World peace*. As religious we cannot be indifferent or remain untouched by conflict and war. We must take a stand, work for world peace, and help those whose lives have been shattered by war.
- *Globalization*. This new attitude to the world opens many perspectives. Intercultural exchanges, international co-operation and cross-border communication create opportunities that were unimaginable in the past. Religious, and especially members of international congregations, can share in the possibilities and contribute to them, giving clear signs of a sense of solidarity that transcends the differences in language, culture, race and country. Religious from different countries who live and work together act as examples in the church and in the world. However, globalization has some negative consequences, too: greater anonymity, marginalization of weaker groups, and new types of poverty. Religious are called upon to stand with people who are victims of globalization.
- *The world of art and culture*. The church has been strongly involved in art and culture, and has a great impact on these areas. It is important to find ways of expressing the Christian message on a cultural level today. Art and culture are typically a personal matter that can never be free of values. Christian values can remain the basis for a Christian culture. Religious are invited to help expand the cultural heritage through a variety of art forms, such as painting, literature and poetry.

• *The world of the media.* The media plays an increasingly important role in society, influencing people's thoughts and actions. There is a great need for religious to remain present in this area, where values are transmitted both consciously and unconsciously. This presence can involve the development of appropriate media circuits through the Internet, radio, television and newspapers, or in making good use of existing secular media channels.

From compassion to charity

These days, many people seem to look down on such attitudes as compassion, charity and the love of one's neighbour. These are seen as being from another age, incompatible with our technical world, which claims that everything can be controlled. Sensitive souls still show compassion and continue to spend time doing charitable works, but they are considered the antithesis of professionals.

As religious we cannot agree with that attitude. Compassion and charity, as expressions of the love of one's neighbour, are related to the core of the gospel message. Compassion is an important feature of God, and charity is human's answer to compassion.

No distant God

The God that we come to know in the Bible, and to whom people of the Christian tradition are devoted, is a God who is very much involved with humankind. Even in the Old Testament, God shows himself to be a sensitive God.

In Exodus we hear God say, "Then the Lord said, 'I have observed the misery of my people who are in Egypt; I have heard their cry on account of their taskmasters. Indeed, I know their sufferings'" (Exodus 3:7). In Hosea we read that God wants to bond with his people: "On that day I will answer, says the Lord, I will answer the heavens and they shall answer the earth" (Hosea 2:21). Later on in the book of Hosea, God becomes even more tender: "Yet it was I who taught Ephraim to walk, I took them up in my arms; but they did not know that I healed them. I led them with cords of human kindness, with bands of love. I was to them like those who lift infants to their cheeks. I bent down to them and fed them" (Hosea 11:3-4).

In the book of Isaiah, we read: "Can a woman forget her nursing child, or show no compassion for the child of her womb? Even these may forget, yet I will not forget you. See, I have inscribed you on the palms of my hands; your walls are continually before me" (Isaiah 49:15-16). "Incline your ear, and come to me; listen, so that you may live. I will make with you an everlasting covenant" (Isaiah 55:3).

The God of the Bible is not at all like the "unmoved mover" described by Aristotle: an insensitive mover who once started everything and who now watches from a distance, like an outsider. The Bible describes God as one who is truly concerned about what happens to humankind and to the world. We might call God "the moved mover."

It is this God whom Jesus talked about and whose example he followed. Jesus, who lived on this earth, is the epitome of God's love of humankind. God is transcendent while at the same time immanent, concerned about the life of each human being – like a mother, a bride, a nurse, a father. It is not without reason that Jesus called God "Abba" or "Father." Jesus had the honour of hearing God say at his baptism: "You are my Son, the Beloved; with you I am well pleased" (Mark 1:11). At critical moments in his life, Jesus spoke to his Abba-Father, and taught us to do the same when he gave us the Our Father. Paul describes the divine fatherhood: "For you did not receive a spirit of slavery to fall back into fear, but you have received a spirit of adoption. When we cry, 'Abba! Father!' it is that very Spirit bearing witness with our spirit that we are children of God" (Romans 8:15-16).

The message that God is concerned about humankind, concerned about how we feel, sensitive like a mother to her child, runs through the Old Testament. Jesus confirmed that message, and brought it to us explicitly. We do not worship a distant God but a God who is worried about us and who allows himself to be touched and moved by our existence. God takes part in our lives through Jesus.

A God who does not exclude anyone

Jesus' life shows us that God is near. The essence of Jesus' message reveals the coming of the kingdom of God: "The time is fulfilled, and the kingdom of God has come near; repent, and believe in the good news" (Mark 1:15). Jesus preached less about himself and more about the coming of the kingdom of God as a place where God is close to humans.

What is the kingdom of God? Some thought it was an earthly rule; during his temptation in the desert, Jesus was indeed offered a worldly empire. That offer was not made by God, but by the tester, Satan. The correct definition of the coming of the kingdom of God is contained in Jesus' response to the question asked by John the Baptist's followers: "Are you the one who is to come, or are we to wait for another?" (Luke 7:19). Jesus answered: "Go and tell John what you have seen and heard: the blind receive their sight, the lame walk, the lepers are cleansed, the deaf hear, the dead are raised, the poor have good news brought to them. And blessed is anyone who takes no offence at me" (Luke 7:22-23).

The description of the kingdom of God in Isaiah's words (Isaiah 58:6 and Isaiah 61:1-2), as used by Jesus, is indeed something that one can take offence at. The Nazarenes took offence when Jesus was in the temple: "He unrolled the scroll and found the place where it was written: 'The Spirit of the Lord is upon me because he has anointed me to bring good news to the poor. He has sent me to proclaim release to the captives and recovery of sight to the blind, to let the oppressed go free, to proclaim the year of the Lord's favour....' Then he began to say to them, 'Today this scripture has been fulfilled in your hearing'" (Luke 4:17-21).

God's reign, the kingdom of God, is coming wherever those poor, hungry and grieving people are treated justly, fed and consoled. The preferential love for the weak and the poor means that God identifies with them in a very special way (Matthew 25). God is revealed in the poor person. The poor person becomes an icon of God! This identification is similar to what Jesus said in the Beatitudes: "Blessed are you who are poor, for yours is the kingdom of God" (Luke 6:20). The kingdom of God shows itself in the poor in a very special way because God identifies with the poor. As Jesus reveals himself in the eucharist, God does so in the poor person.

Yet God does not exclude anyone; the preferential character of God's love is an illustration of its universality. We can all benefit from God's love, but only if the abandoned and forgotten benefit from it first. They are always the first to be excluded, ignored and neglected.

This last sentence captures Vincent de Paul's expression that "the poor were his masters" because they are all too often the oppressed. They must be promoted to the rank of master to be at the same level as others.

The kingdom of God breaks through

Jesus did not only preach about God's preferential love for the poor, he also demonstrated it through the choices he made, the positions he took, the miracles he performed. He always stood on the side of the poor. By healing them and by washing away their sins, he wanted to make room for God in their hearts, minds and souls. He wanted to say, through his words and actions, that the power of evil, which hurts a person's body and mind, should not have the final word. God's kingdom must break through where humans feel that they can become children of God.

That is what happened in the case of Zacchaeus, who had to go through a conversion process to be able to do what Jesus described as the kingdom of God: "Look, half of my possessions, Lord, I will give to the poor; and if I have defrauded anyone of anything, I will pay back four times as much" (Luke 19:8).

The kingdom of God cannot happen only in the future. It must happen here and now, abundantly. This immediacy and abundance is illustrated by the miracle of the loaves and fish that resulted in twelve full baskets of leftovers. All of Jesus' miracles demonstrate the abundance of which humans seem incapable. Everything is made inferior to that abundance, even the law. Jesus does not abolish the law (he does not even want to change it), but it is given its rightful place, subordinated on the law of love.

The kingdom of God breaks through when God's love appears in the world, and not when all the rules and regulations are being followed. That is the meaning of Jesus' answer to the lawyer's question regarding the most important commandment: it is love. Everything must be fulfilled according to the law of the love of God and of our neighbour. The commandment of love is more important than all the rest when people's salvation, life and healing are at stake.

The kingdom of God overcomes us

The coming of the kingdom of God needs a commitment. It influences humans completely, forces us to turn our whole lives upside down, like Zacchaeus did. It cannot wait until tomorrow, until next year, or until the hereafter to take shape in our lives. The kingdom of God, which has an eschatological dimension that refers to the time when God will be all in everyone, must start now: "The time is fulfilled, and the kingdom of God has come near; repent, and believe in the good news" (Mark 1:15). We are called to repent, to experience *metanoia*, to distance ourselves definitively and fundamentally from our old self, and to become a new type of person. We must "put a hand to the plough and not look back" (Luke 9:62).

All is concentrated on the double commandment of love. Our relationship with God is summarized in the first part: "You shall love the Lord your God with all your heart, and with all your soul, and with all your mind. This is the greatest and first commandment" (Matthew 22:37-38). This excerpt expresses our passion for God. God, who loves humans passionately, desires love that is just as passionate. There are two dimensions to that interaction with God: praying, through which humans address God, and the celebration of the sacraments, which is more a gesture from God to humans.

The first part of the double commandment is followed by the call to love our neighbour as ourselves. We could say that the love of God is not real and honest until it is focused on the love of our neighbour. Our passion for God, and God's passion for us, must evolve and become a passion for humans, and it must result in charity. The ethics that this process can generate must be a reflection of God's love. As one expression put it, "If humans can be so good, then how good God must be!"

The love of our fellow beings becomes a prophetic testimony of God's love and of the kingdom of God. The kingdom of God becomes visible in our concrete love for our others. Shaping God's passion is being a light for the world: "You are the light of the world. A city built on a hill cannot be hidden ... In the same way, let your light shine before others, so that they may see your good works and give glory to your Father in heaven" (Matthew 5:14-16). It is through our good works that we bear witness to God's glory, helping to establish the kingdom of God in our world.

Walking in Jesus' footsteps – thinking like him, listening to him – bears witness to his words during the Last Supper: "I give you a new commandment, that you love one another. Just as I have loved you, you also should love one another" (John 13:34). In his first letter, John comments on Jesus' own witness: "We know love by this, that he laid down his life for us – and we ought to lay down our lives for one another …" (1 John 3:16) for "since God loved us so much, we also ought to love one another" (1 John 4:11).

God's love precedes our ethics and our actions of love, and strengthens our ethics. It becomes clear that only when our love of God is given hands and feet will our commitment to the poor, the weak and the needy become authentic. Our passion for God leads to our passion for humans, and eventually turns from compassion to charity.

Passion for others

To support our reflection on our passion for others, we will explore the gospel passage in which Jesus' answer regarding the most important commandment is followed by the story of the Good Samaritan (Luke 10:25-37). This parable serves as the basis for every reflection on charity and on ethics as actions of love.

The passage starts with a question from the lawyer who asked Jesus which was the most important commandment. Eventually (because Jesus invited him to do so) he provided the answer himself. His answer contains no new information since it appears in the Old Testament: "Hear, O Israel: The Lord is our God, the Lord alone. You shall love the Lord your God with all your heart, and with all your soul, and with all your might" (Deuteronomy 6:4-5). And in Leviticus we find the second part: "You shall not take vengeance or bear a grudge against any of your people, but you shall love your neighbour as yourself: I am the Lord" (Leviticus 19:18). The fact that the lawyer quoted these two passages proves that, even before Jesus, the double commandment existed. Jesus did not invent the double commandment, but he did place this commandment above all other rules and regulations. This tells us that we must follow all rules and regulations in the spirit of the commandment of love.

The lawyer then asked the famous question: "And who is my neighbour?" (Luke 10:29). Let us take a closer look at the parable in order to get a clearer picture of the charity that we are asked to live.

Three people are on their way, becoming more themselves through the fulfillment of their roles. We can recognize ourselves in them. First, a priest and a Levite pass by. They are two people who hold special offices in the Jewish religion: the priest conducts the religious service, and the Levite preaches. You would expect both of them to know and follow the Torah very closely, showing through their example how to live in a way that is pleasing to God. The priest is on duty and therefore cannot soil himself with blood. He follows the rules very strictly and ignores the suffering of another human being. He is living proof of the mentality against which Jesus struggled, a mentality that still exists today. It is doing everything by the book, doing whatever people expect us to do, and being glad about it. It is also the mentality of task division: that is not for me to do; we cannot do it all, can we! There are groups and organizations whose sole purpose is to solve such a problem. It is also fear of the unknown: why was this man attacked? Is this perhaps an ambush? Is he playing some sort of game? They should have organized better supervision or installed better lighting (to speak in today's terms).

The Levite knows the law because he teaches it. He is familiar with Leviticus and with the obligation to love his neighbour as himself. But maybe he has to be in the temple on time in order to teach the people. Maybe he has everything planned very nicely. He, too, has several reasons to continue on his way and not to stop. However, those two men have seen the victim. They have seen him lying stretched out on the ground, but they pass by him, ignore him, avoid looking into his face. Their eyes do not meet the eyes of the wounded man.

Their (and our) attitude seems reasonable, but it overlooks the commandment of love:

- I do not have time;
- I have another task to fulfil;
- I cannot do it all;
- There are organizations to solve that kind of problem;
- Maybe it was his own fault that he was attacked;
- I am not trained to help that person;
- I have another appointment that I cannot miss;
- I have retired; that is something for young people to deal with;
- I am not paid to do that.

There are other types of reasoning that can be added.

In all those cases, we close our eyes to the situation of the other person and refuse to let ourselves be touched by his or her suffering because we want to carry on with our own well-planned life. But then along comes that stranger, that man from Samaria. The Jews despise the Samaritans for allegedly being unfaithful, for praying in another temple. It is remarkable that Jesus chose for this story two "exemplary" Jews, a priest and a Levite, and juxtaposed them with an "unfaithful" person. The Samaritan was most likely a traveller, while the two others were simply on their way to work. He noticed the injured man and "and when he saw him, he was moved with pity" (Luke 10:33). Here we find an important detail: the Samaritan notices the other person and allows himself to be moved by the face of the stranger lying wounded on the ground.

By allowing himself to be moved, he makes it possible for a bond of solidarity to be created between himself and the victim. The other person, the victim, enters his life unasked, and chooses to look at the victim's face. His travel schedule is affected by that stranger. He can choose to leave the wounded person where he is lying, reasoning that he has nothing to do with that man, that he does not want to be disturbed. Or he can choose to put aside his autonomy and drive for self-fulfillment and let the other enter his existence.

The Samaritan's attitude challenges my drive for self-fulfillment, a topic on which so much has been written lately. It is seen as each person's right to fulfill himself or herself, and to make his or her choices independently. This touches on a person's freedom, which is considered to be the greatest gift of all, and which is used to make self-fulfillment possible. I have the right to pursue my own life, and to live it to the full. I wish to make well-considered choices; to do that, I require a certain amount of freedom. All that might hinder me, including my fellow humans, must be avoided so that I can actualize myself.

Many egocentric people are wrapped up in their own existence and surround themselves with forms of spirituality to give them fulfillment. "I am entitled to spare time; I am entitled to a sufficient portion of culture; I have the right to build up a meaningful life," they may say. Victor Frankl teaches us that humans can only find meaning in their lives when they have a project outside themselves. They must have a goal to which they are committed and that gives them satisfaction. The gospel goes even further, stating a paradox: "Those who try to make their life secure will lose it, but those who lose their life will keep it" (Luke 17:33), and "No one has greater love than this, to lay down one's life for one's friends" (John 15:13). The commitment to the other becomes a condition for finding real life: we must break out of the vicious circle of self-love, allowing another person to enter our lives unasked to break it for us. And as we connect our life with the fate of the other, the gates to self-realization open.

The Samaritan allows himself to be touched and moved in a way that puts a restriction on his own unlimited freedom. Although he can say "no" to the unheard request for help from this stranger, instead he chooses to say "yes."

That is the core of our solidarity, and it is where charity begins. The other invites me to respond without actually giving me an order. Since I am free, I can say "no," unless I let the other's presence take precedence over my own freedom. Then I cannot say "no."

The Samaritan does not allow himself to be ruled by his own freedom. He takes his freedom into his own hands and decides to become a neighbour to this unknown fellow human. And then the miracle of passion blossoms and grows into charity.

- "He interrupted his journey." The person who crosses his path becomes more important than his schedule. Is my fellow human being more important in my life than my schedule, my rest?
- "He went up to him." He moves towards his fellow human, who is in distress. He does not wait for his fellow human to knock on his door and beg for help. Do I see the poor around me, and do I go out to them?
- "He bandaged his wounds, having poured oil and wine on them." He approaches the other with what he possesses, and is creative in his care. Do I hide behind the excuse of a lack of means, knowledge or equipment?
- "Then he put him on his own animal." He shares the property he possesses at that moment. Am I prepared to share my house, my possessions, my books?
- "Brought him to an inn, and took care of him." He finds an adequate place to nurse his fellow human. Do I find places, and do I use my time, to support my neighbour?
- "The next day." He adapts his itinerary to the needs of the stranger.
- "He took out two denarii, gave them to the innkeeper." He shares what little he has with the one who suffers.
- "Take care of him; and when I come back, I will repay you whatever more you spend." His love becomes truly boundless, and he is prepared to spend even more money. Do we still dare to take risks in our lives?

The Samaritan's behaviour gives rise to many questions and confronts us with the truth of charity. It is universal, not aimed at receiving favours in return, not aimed at gratitude, not aimed at obtaining a reward in the hereafter. He became the neighbour of this total stranger because he "showed him mercy" (Luke 10:37). And then Jesus spoke again: "Go and do likewise" (Luke 10:37). That says it all.

9

Growing Older

The statistics regarding religious in Western countries do not lie: we are growing older. In many religious orders and congregations, the average age is over 70. Individual religious, as well as the community, have to face that reality. In the past, the various age groups were represented equally in religious communities, but today the majority consists of elderly brothers or sisters.

That fact may affect us negatively or even paralyze us. In some groups, the only people that are still being taken care of are the elderly members of the community themselves. However, we can deal with this new reality in a positive way. We are called to live this particular phase of life, which follows an active apostolate phase, as positively as possible and without neglecting our role as religious. Along the way, we may need to develop a new spirituality, that of the aging religious.

Our current views on aging

In 1982, the United Nations organized the first World Assembly on Aging, which took place in Vienna. This gathering offered a clear description of the aging person in contemporary society in order to develop a common view on the place of the elderly. Let us review some data from the action plan as a basis for our reflection on the aging religious.

In 1950, the elderly world population was 8%; it increased to 10% in 2000. Estimates show that by the year

2050, 21% of the people on this planet will be over 60 years old. By the year 2150, that ratio will be one in three. There has been a steady increase in the number of elderly people who are in need of special care, too. This is also a common phenomenon in many convents.

Some of the conclusions that were drawn at the first assembly on aging are positive. For example, the elderly are bound to become human capital that must not be underestimated. They need to be given the chance of participating in what is happening in the world. The healthy elderly can contribute considerably to the economy and to social life.

Much importance is given to where one grows old, because this may determine how elderly people continue to function and may have an impact on their general well-being. Finally, young people are invited to pay more attention to the elderly, on both a human and a professional level.

During the International Year of the Elderly in 1999, similar suggestions were put forth. A plea was made for mutual understanding, harmony and assistance between generations, and for the recognition of elderly people's invaluable contributions to their families' lives, community and country. Nations were asked to take the elderly into account, and all social sectors were encouraged to listen to them.

In short, the current view on the aging process is characterized by attention to the positive abilities and contributions made by elderly people. They deserve a place on all levels of society. Our society, which is evolving ever more quickly, is asked to reduce its pace so that elderly people are able to participate. These suggestions have far-reaching consequences for elderly religious, also.

While congregations used to devote most of their attention to the work done by active religious, that work being the congregation's showpiece, they now have to consider consecrated life in all its different aspects. In the past, one or two young religious would take care of the few elderly members of their community – the communities consisting of a majority of young religious and only a few elderly religious. Today, that care has become a full-time task for the few remaining young religious – sometimes even their main task.

In the past, a religious would be expected to remain active in the apostolate as long as possible. Quite often, religious would continue to work in the apostolate as volunteers until they were no longer able to carry on physically with their work. Today, it has become common practice for religious to end their apostolate once they have retired officially. Some of them, wanting to work as volunteers, seek out or are given new missions that have nothing to do with their traditional apostolate.

In several countries, orders and congregations have taken measures to provide proper care of their members who have special needs. The statement made at the second World Assembly on Aging, held in Madrid in 2002, states: "In the 20th century, old age was but a footnote. In the 21st century, however, it is to become the main theme." We can apply this statement to the world of the religious as well.

I wish to focus on the question of how individual religious are to respond, in an evangelical way, to the fact of growing older. Is there such a thing as a spirituality of aging that we can develop, and can it inspire other elderly people?

The fact of growing old

In the Bible we find several texts that explain the meaning and significance of growing old. In Leviticus we read, "You shall rise before the aged, and defer to the old; and you shall fear your God" (Leviticus 19:32). And the book of Deuteronomy says: "Honour your father and your mother, as the Lord your God commanded you" (Deuteronomy 5:16). The entire third chapter of Ecclesiasticus deals with the respect we owe to our parents, especially when they are old (see Sirach 3:12-13).

These texts certainly invite us to respect the elderly and to support them when they have grown weak and require special care. Psalm 92 contains praise for those who continue to seek inspiration from God: "They are planted in the house of the Lord; they flourish in the courts of our God. In old age they still produce fruit; they are always green and full of sap" (Psalm 92:13-14). This text is often linked with the elderly in the Bible who are called by God: for example, Abraham and Sarah, who at an advanced age became the ancestors of the people of Israel; and Zechariah and Elizabeth, who become the parents of John the Baptist when they are long past their youth.

Old people are described as sages as in Psalm 90: "So teach us to count our days that we may gain a wise heart" (Psalm 90:12). But the reality of growing older, and the physical limitations and decline that this holds, cannot be denied. "Vanity of vanities, says the Teacher; all is vanity" (Ecclesiastes 12:8). And he refers to the aging person who decays slowly: "All must go to their eternal home, and the mourners will go about the streets" (Ecclesiastes 12:5).

In the New Testament, Jesus' disciples seemed to have had very little time to talk about the process of aging. Figures such as Anna and Simeon are presented as wise people to whom others are to listen respectfully. In the letters, we are told to treat our elders with respect: "'Honour your father and mother' – this is the first commandment with a promise: 'so that it may be well with you and you may live long on the earth'" (Ephesians 6:2-3). A moral code is imposed on the elders: "Tell the older men to be temperate, serious, prudent, and sound in faith, in love, and in endurance. Likewise, tell the older women to be reverent in behaviour, not to be slanderers or slaves to drink; they are to teach what is good" (Titus 2:2-3).

Through John we hear Jesus' magnificent words encouraging us to accept our new life situation: "Very truly, I tell you, when you were younger, you used to fasten your own belt and to go wherever you wished. But when you grow old, you will stretch out your hands, and someone else will fasten a belt around you and take you where you do not wish to go" (John 21:18). It is this last passage that should shape the attitude of elderly people towards the rest of the world. This attitude is characterized by receptiveness and acceptance, or the willingness to let go of the control of their own lives and to put their trust in other people and in God.

A number of church documents also deal with elderly people, appealing to the faithful to adopt the aforementioned evangelical attitude towards them. In *Familiaris Consortio*, Pope John Paul II asks that the elderly be given a place at the heart of the family and of society; he also underlines the value of process of aging.

> There are cultures which manifest a unique veneration and great love for the elderly: far from being outcasts from the family or merely tolerated as a useless burden, they continue to be present and to take an active and responsible part in family life, though having to respect the autonomy of the new family; above all they carry out the important mission of being a witness to the past and a source of wisdom for the young and for the future.[50]

Other cultures, however, especially in the wake of industrial and urban development, have set the elderly aside in unacceptable ways. This causes acute suffering to them and spiritually impoverishes many families.

The pastoral activity of the church must help everyone to discover and to benefit from the role of the elderly within the civil and ecclesial community, in particular within the family. In fact, the process of aging helps to clarify a range of human values; it shows the continuity of generations and marvellously demonstrates the interdependence of

God's people. The elderly often have the charism to bridge generation gaps: how many children and young people have found understanding and love in the eyes and words and caresses of the aging? And how many old people have willingly subscribed to the inspired word that "Grandchildren are the crown of the aged, and the glory of children is their parents" (Proverbs 17:6)?

During the International Year of the Elderly, a document entitled "The Dignity of Older People and Their Mission in the Church and in the World" discussed the significance of growing older. It also described the charisms of growing older: disinterestedness, memory, experience, interdependence, and a more complete vision of life.

During the first World Assembly on Aging, the pope's message was repeated as the basis of a policy regarding elderly people:

> Life is a gift of God to man who is created out of love in the image and likeness of God. This understanding of the sacred dignity of the human person leads to the appreciation of every stage of life. It is a question of consistency and justice. It is impossible to truly value the life of an older person if the life of a child is not valued from the moment of its conception. No one knows where we might arrive, if life is no longer respected as something inalienable and sacred.[51]

A number of concerns are identified in that document: the marginalization of the elderly, the lack of facilities and the absence of proper care for older people, the absence of adapted employment or training for elderly people, and the impossibility for many elderly people to lead an active social life. A proper pastoral plan for aging people needs to be developed. The document *Christifidelis Laici* treats the subject of older people and the gift of wisdom:

I now address older people, oftentimes unjustly considered as unproductive, if not directly an insupportable burden. I remind older people that the Church calls and expects them to continue to exercise their mission in the apostolic and missionary life. This is not only a possibility for them, but it is their duty even in this time in their life when age itself provides opportunities in some specific and basic way.

The Bible delights in presenting the older person as the symbol of someone rich in wisdom and fear of the Lord (cf. Sir 25:4-6). In this sense the "gift" of older people can be specifically that of being the witness to tradition in the faith both in the Church and in society (cf. Ps 44: 2; Ex 12:26-27), the teacher of the lessons of life (cf. Sir 6:34; 8:11-12), and the worker of charity.

At this moment the growing number of older people in different countries worldwide and the expected retirement of persons from various professions and the workplace provides older people with a new opportunity in the apostolate. Involved in the task is their determination to overcome the temptation of taking refuge in a nostalgia in a never-to-return past or fleeing from present responsibility because of difficulties encountered in a world of one novelty after another. They must always have a clear knowledge that one's role in the Church and society does not stop at a certain age at all, but at such times knows only new ways of application. As the Psalmist says: "They still bring forth fruit in old age, they are ever full of sap and green, to show that the Lord is upright" (Ps 92:15-16). I repeat all that I said during the celebration of the Older People's Jubilee: "Arriving at an older age is to be considered a privilege: not simply because not everyone has the good fortune to reach this stage in life, but also, and above all, because this period provides real possibilities for better evaluating the past, for knowing and living more deeply the Paschal Mystery, for becoming an example in the Church for the whole People of God ...." (CL, 48)

This text is an excellent summary of how we as religious can look at the fact of growing older from a biblical perspective.

Towards a spirituality of aging

Given their specific vocation and consecrated lifestyle, religious can give meaning to that phase of their life in a very personal way. And thus they can inspire other elderly people. Let us explore a number of patterns of a well-founded spirituality for the elderly.

Developing our own humanness

Sometimes we hear people say that religious never retire; they only change their occupations after they have retired officially. It is important for religious to consider their official retirement as a transition to a new phase in life in which they continue their journey with God in a different way.

In the gospel we find proof that humans are never too old to receive a visit from God. The day of one's retirement can be a time when God sends an angel with a message of love and an invitation to respond in a new way. Maybe our daily preoccupations have prevented us from giving God the foremost place in our lives. Maybe we have been busy focusing on ourselves instead of our neighbour or God as we fulfilled our apostolate. This new life phase may be an opportunity to shift the emphasis in our lives: freed from one specific task, we may suddenly have energy to spare.

Many brothers and sisters had become one with their apostolate. Their work was everything to them and every friendship was linked to their work; they were appreciated as a result of the function that they filled. We all know religious who thought they had many friends, but when the time came to retire, they realized that they had been respected because of their position. For those brothers and sisters, this double loss was difficult. Over time they developed new friendships with people who appreciated them for themselves.

There are many needs; the challenge is finding ways to meet them. These needs are invitations for religious to remain active after their official retirement. They can become active, and remain so, if their activities are outlined clearly. They can give advice but must be careful not to moralize. They will experience the loneliness of growing old but at the same time have a social network. These are a number of paradoxes that may arise in their lives.

On the other hand, we find religious who resist giving up their activities, who refuse to appoint a successor, who wish to die on the field of honour. Are consecrated people called to realize this ideal? Is that not clinging to life, to one's honour, to one's work? How far have such people strayed from the paradoxical gospel text: "Those who find their life will lose it, and those who lose their life for my sake will find it" (Matthew 10:39).

Often such people are afraid to face with themselves; they keep on running from themselves, seeking solace in their work. Upon their retirement, they fall into an abyss because they have forgotten that work was only one way of approaching God and their neighbour, one way of making God's love visible and tangible on this earth. But the love of God can be experienced and passed on in various ways, as we will see below.

We develop types of passivity

As we grow older, we are invited to let go, aware that we can live our lives to the full only if we are willing to do so. Due to our more limited abilities, the result of the aging process, we are forced to open our hands and let go of the things to which we once clung.

Until this point, we may claim that we expect everything from God but worked to bring about our own security in life. Our active life may have been an illusion of our claim that life is given by God's hand, in which we devote ourselves to the redemption of others. Now that we are older, we are freed of the illusion of being able to manage everything ourselves, to realize our own salvation.

When we confront our own weakness, when our strength diminishes, we are invited to face our faith attitude, not only theoretically but in practice. Our weakness becomes an external grace that helps us to receive God's grace fully. After all, it is God who is responsible for our salvation, not us! In that light, it is much easier to understand Paul as he speaks about the thorn that is tormenting him but eventually becomes his salvation:

> Therefore, to keep me from being too elated, a thorn was given to me in the flesh, a messenger of Satan to torment me, to keep me from being too elated. Three times I appealed to the Lord about this, that it would leave me, but he said to me, "My grace is sufficient for you, for power is made perfect in weakness." So, I will boast all the more gladly of my weaknesses, so that the power of Christ may dwell in me. Therefore I am content with weaknesses, insults, hardships, persecutions and calamities for the sake of Christ; for whenever I am weak, then I am strong. (2 Corinthians 12:7-10)

That is the kind of passivity that I mean: being able to respond in a positive way to whatever faces us, and to discover the path that we are meant to follow. It is accepting and living John's message: "Very truly, I tell you, when you were younger, you used to fasten your own belt and to go wherever you wished. But when you grow old, you will stretch out your hands, and someone else will fasten a belt around you and take you where you do not wish to go" (John 21:18). Is that not the essence of our vocation: shifting the stress from ourselves to God? We stretch out our hands when we open them to the grace of the moment. Jesus described the fragility of life when he talked about the flowers in the fields: "And why do you worry about clothing? Consider the lilies of the field, how they grow; they neither toil nor spin, yet I tell you, even Solomon in all his glory was not clothed like one of these" (Matthew 6:28-29).

This life phase is an invitation to deal with time differently. The expression "time is money" has made its way into our convents, too. Religious from the east and the south often remark, "All you westerners think about is work. You forget to enjoy life!" The Trappist monk Thomas Merton said, "One can only become a spiritual being if one does no longer feel guilty about not doing anything productive."[52] Due to our exaggerated activities, we may well have neglected our primary mission in life: becoming spiritual beings who are completely open to God and our neighbour. As we try to deal with our time differently, we may wonder whether we indeed reserve the best of our time for God, and whether we devote ourselves to others as we should. When retired religious have time only to develop themselves – to do their hobbies and to keep physically fit, for example – then they have strayed far from their vocation. In that case, they are pursuing their own ambitions in order to actualize themselves: whereas in the past they would try to actualize themselves through their work, today they may try to do so through cultural activities and hobbies. I am not saying that apostolic religious should lead a completely contemplative life once they have retired. On the contrary, they are called to become apostolic by adding a deeper dimension to their relationship with God and with their neighbour. A confrere once told me: "Ever since I retired, I feel as I felt at the start of my religious life. I can spend my time taking care of poor people, and thus my praying becomes everlasting praise and gratitude to the Lord, represented by my neighbour."

Another brother told me, "As I became involved in palliative care, I discovered the true meaning of compassion. It has to do with making time, with being there for people. In the past I never had time, I was always busy, and never really present. This is the most grace-filled period of my life."

An atmosphere of gratitude

Aging religious should also be grateful: grateful for the life of their congregation and grateful for their own lives. In some cases, we are talking about an era that is coming to an end. There are no more successors in the order's own ranks, and the apostolates are passed on to others. There may be regrets about this situation. And some religious may be critical of the people who run the apostolates now, saying, "In our day, it was all much better. See how they waste time and money. And what about the Christian identity?" There are reasons to grieve, but there are just as many reasons to be grateful for the good that has happened due to the congregation, and for the good that is still happening today, albeit in another context. We should also be grateful for our own past, recognizing that we have been instruments in God's hands. We may give over our faults to God's mercy. The following quote from A. Roland Holst's poem "De Ploeger" ("The Ploughman") fits this situation:

> I do not demand a harvest, for I have no granaries.
> I am at your service, without property.
> But I am rich in that
> I may pull the plough that is your Word,
> And in that you have given me,
> This remote country and these
> High meadows where – as I take my lunch,
> Leaning against the horses of my will and keeping silent –
> I can see the sea stretched out before me.

Teilhard de Chardin put it this way: "I experience the loving will of God at the tip of the pen that I use to write, at the edge of the blade of the shovel that I use to break the soil, at the tip of the tongue that I use to speak."[53] Blessed are those who can maintain that attitude until the end of their lives.

Gratitude should also characterize our relationship with the young religious who still surround us. Instead of focusing on the weaknesses, faults and differences that we notice in them, we do better to devote our attention to the things that we have in common, especially our charism, which they sustain and modernize. In communities dominated by conflicts caused by the generation gap, it is most often the elderly religious who do not succeed in showing understanding for the behaviour of young religious, even though the wisdom of the elders could help to narrow that gap or even bridge it.

Dealing with suffering

In a conference for religious held in Kinshasa in 1980, Pope John Paul II said,

> How could I forget about the sick, invalid and elderly sisters? In the course of the day and even at night, when they cannot get to sleep, they offer the Lord the silent sacrifice of their almost uninterrupted prayer, which is their physical and moral suffering, of their approval of God's divine will. They are the priestly people that Christ made his through the blood of the cross. With him they are saving the world.[54]

The mystery of suffering can take us by surprise, but it can also place us in solidarity with Christ and all who suffer.

First, we have to learn to accept suffering and loss as part of life. Just because we are deteriorating physically does not mean that our selves are decaying, too. There is more to us than the way we look.

I once read a story about an elderly lady who, holding a picture of herself at the age of five, said: "Do you see that pretty girl with her blond braids? Well, that's me. I was five at the time. I do not have the impression that I have changed. Something in me is ageless. Of course, that little girl has grown up and has grown old, but the person that she was and still is hasn't changed. Everything in me has grown old, but I myself have not. What you see of me is but a mask." This lady did not deny the fact that she has grown old, and she did not need special makeup to conceal her reality. An elderly brother once said "My cancer is my apostolate." He understood that God continued to call him and to send him through the various stages of his life. At that moment he could imitate Christ as the Suffering Servant and thus take part in redemption. It is, to quote Paul, experiencing that mysterious message: "I am now rejoicing in my sufferings for your sake, and in my flesh I am completing what is lacking in Christ's afflictions for the sake of his body, that is, the church" (Colossians 1:24).

Rainer Maria Rilke has described our way of dealing with suffering as follows:

> Be patient toward all that is unsolved in your heart and to try to love the questions themselves like locked rooms and like books that are written in a very foreign tongue. Do not now seek the answers, which cannot be given you because you would not be able to live them. And the point is, to live everything. Live the questions now. Perhaps you will then gradually, without noticing it, live along some distant day into the answer.[55]

People who succeed in dealing with their own suffering will also succeed in opening up to the suffering of others. That is true compassion, which is a way of life, rather than something that one can learn. We hope that religious become the ultimate compassionate people.

New models in the gospel

Finally, we may invite elderly religious to imitate the models and stories from the gospel that best fit their new phase in life. Reflecting on the example of Jesus, who withdrew to be alone with his Father, may result in making more time to pray. Or we might consider Jesus who went to spend time in the company of his friends Martha, Mary and Lazarus, and who praised Mary for having chosen the better part (Luke 10:38-45); our response may involve being with our confreres more consciously and listening more intensely to the stories of people in distress.

But we can also choose certain personalities from the gospel who represent the elderly, such as Zechariah, Elizabeth, Simeon and Anna. They are all confident, patient and hopeful about the coming of the Messiah; they contemplate the Lord through prayer and meditation. Elderly religious can likewise be hopeful and confident that the kingdom of God will break through one day, thus allowing it to break through in their lives.

Now I understand the brother who, celebrating his jubilee, insisted on quoting Simeon during the celebrations. Three weeks later we were together again for his funeral. "Master, now you are dismissing your servant in peace, according to your word; for my eyes have seen your salvation, which you have prepared in the presence of all peoples, a light for revelation to the Gentiles and for glory to your people Israel" (Luke 2:29-32).

10

Vocations

Not long ago, I was struck by this remark: "To be honest, I do not see why we should continue to develop pastoral initiatives concerning vocations. A vocation is the work of God, after all. If we, as religious, live a good life, then the appeal of that life should be enough to convince young people to join our communities."

Obviously, I agree that vocations are first of all the work of God. God takes the initiative; God is the first to speak. We also understand that, if we wish to attract new blood, our religious life and our community life must be appealing and attractive. The first Christians knew this: "See how good it is to live together as brothers and sisters" (Psalm 133); as Tertullian put it, "See ... how they love one another."[56] It is true that praying for vocations remains a priority and that those who suffer can sacrifice their lives to stimulate the number of vocations.

So it is important to continue to pay attention to our personal religious life and to try to make our communities schools of love. If we say, like Jesus did, "Come and see" (John 1:39), then something that is worthwhile seeing should be visible. However, all this should not stop us from taking initiatives to stimulate the number of vocations. After all, God uses people to carry on his work on earth, including encouraging vocations. The development of pastoral care of vocations needs to be seen as a type of service to the young, to the church and to the poor. It being a kind of service makes pastoral care of vocations legitimate. It makes it an affair that concerns all of us.

Pastoral care of vocations as a type of service

Our chief concern when developing the pastoral care of vocations is not the preservation or increase of the number of brothers and sisters in our congregations. Clearly, a minimum number of religious is necessary to fulfill the mission of the congregation. But the most important motivation for making ourselves known as a congregation or order is the type of service that we wish to provide to the young, the church and the world. Let us look at this in more depth.

A service to the young

Reflecting on our own vocation to religious life, we realize that it was an individual or a group of people who appealed to us at a certain moment and who opened the perspective on a religious life. Could we not say that this person or this group of people was the medium used by God to let us hear God's voice? We may refer to the biblical story of Eli and Samuel as an example of this form of communication. Eli was not perfect – quite the contrary – but for Samuel he became God's medium, God's voice. It was God who called. Eli grew convinced of that too, having heard him calling several times. However, Samuel required Eli's intervention to understand what God was asking of him and to find the right words to answer God's call. So people do not need to be perfect in order to be used by God as his voice. We know that God writes straight with crooked lines. Everyone can become Eli in the story of another person's vocation.

Young people need to hear the voice of God through their neighbour. If we keep silent, we may prevent God from speaking through us. God's word and teachings, in combination with our example and our service, are the ingredients of authentic pastoral care of vocations.

What stands out for me in the story of my vocation? Was it what a brother said to me, at exactly the right time? Was it the sincerity with which I witnessed some brothers living their lives and doing their work? Was it the service of a brother who did not consider himself too good to serve food in the refectory? It was only later, however, that I learned that our founder said, "I am to live as a true example for you. I am to teach you and I am to serve you."[57]

During a recent visit to Rwanda, I attended the profession of several sisters. The bishop, who was presiding, lived the Eucharist so intensely that many of the participants were moved by it. He lived the Eucharist; he was the Eucharist.

There is another example that I will never forget. One day, a doctor was asked to explain what religious life was all about, especially religious life as lived by a Brother of Charity. The doctor had been working for the Brothers of Charity for many years, but the question surprised him nonetheless. So he pointed to a brother who was close by and said, "Observe this man and you will know what a Brother of Charity stands for." The brother to whom the doctor had pointed was a very spiritual man. He was the kind of man who lived his life smiling, trying to discover the good in every individual. He was a humble man, a man who was always prepared to serve other people. He was a man who lived his vocation to the full. He was real.

Young people are in need of people who proclaim the word of God and who live up to it without any compromises. They need people who are willing to live a life of service in imitation of Jesus. That is how we are to demonstrate what it means to have a vocation these days. Young people need to discover their own vocation through people who live their vocation as Christians in the world or as religious, and who thus fulfill their lives.

Through acting as examples, speaking the word of God, and serving other people, religious are to show how they try to realize their vocation to live a holy life. Nothing less, nothing more. That was the point of view of Vatican II, and it was also described and put into practice by Francis of Sales. It is a point that we are invited to adopt. Every Christian is called upon to live a life of holiness and to live his or her baptismal grace to the full. There are many ways to do this: as a lay person in the world, as a consecrated person, as a priest, in married life or in celibacy. Everyone is called upon to discover his or her unique way of life.

It is important for young people to learn to discover their own vocation through word, example and service. They must learn how they can achieve holiness by living the message of the gospel and how they can give shape to their vocation. We who, through our words and deeds, are allowed to address the young need to realize that we are also instruments in God's hands. Each of us has to live our vocation to the full in order to be able to offer to the young this whole range of ways in which one can fulfill one's vocation. Only through living one's laity consistently can one help the young to discover that they are called upon to live a life of laity in the world, and that laity is their way of achieving holiness. The same is true for priests, consecrated people and married people.

A vocation as such may be universal, but the way in which one gives shape to it is unique and complementary. We must keep this in mind as we organize our pastoral care of vocations. We need to take into account the universal vocation to holiness that is expressed in the way God has called upon us. Our openness with regard to other vocations is not irreconcilable with the way in which we live our own vocation. If we were to speak only about the universal vocation without making any mention of our own vocation, we would not be making a very authentic impression. If we were to speak only about our own vocation without making room for a more universal vocation, we would prove to be rather narrow-minded and give the impression of superiority. Obviously, I have the right to consider my own vocation the best for myself, as long as I am willing to understand that others have the same rights.

In fact, as religious, we demonstrate to young people that God's unconditional love can satisfy a human life and that it can make someone extremely happy. Young people have the right to hear this message from authentic and enthusiastic religious who can only explain their joy in life on the basis of the gift of God's love in their lives.

It is that authenticity, that enthusiasm that may be contagious and become the root of a longing in others to give shape to their lives in the same way. But even that is only partly the work of humans. God sets off with humans without excluding them.

A type of service to the church

Time and again, I am moved by that beautiful image Paul used when he compared the church to a body with many members. Every part of that body has its own unique vocation, is necessary, and serves to preserve the body as a whole.

Similarly, the vocation to live a consecrated life may be regarded as a necessary part of a whole. Every order and congregation introduced something new at a certain point in time and made its own unique contribution to help to develop that body.

That much remains true in our times as well. A congregation or order must not think too quickly that its task is accomplished. What a void villagers experience when the last of the sisters leaves. That void has nothing to do with the work that is no longer being done. It is about a living testimonial of God's love in a world where this love is so often covered up.

One day, the Archbishop of Ranchi, Cardinal Toppo, said to me, "You introduce something new in the church. For so long I had dreamed about founding a congregation of brothers and to do something for the handicapped.

And now that you have arrived, young people get the opportunity to fulfill their vocation in life as a brother. By taking care of chronic psychiatric patients, they show yet another dimension of Jesus to the world: his concern for the underprivileged."

In Ukraine, we are facing similar challenges: promoting the vocation of brother in an extremely clerical church and giving shape to the apostolic dimension of the gospel by taking care of children with disabilities in a church that focuses primarily on the liturgy.

A church in which the dimension of consecrated life is absent is a limited church, a church that lacks an essential part. Given that religious, as a result of their liminal sensibility, are often among the first to react to new emergency situations, a world without religious would be deprived of the creative dynamism of the church. I am saying all this without pretence. I am only elaborating on the image of a body with many members, as introduced by Paul.

When contemporary religious take pastoral initiatives to stimulate vocations, they do so because they believe that they were blessed with a charism – not to put it in earthenware pots and to bury it in the ground, but to share it with other people. Pastoral care of vocations is an act of faith. Today, religious still have the task of focusing on a part of the gospel and becoming prophetic in the church and in the world.

Consecrated people like to be described as people who are not afraid to go out on the edge, to places where people are hurt, abused and deprived of their dignity, in order to proclaim the word of hope drawn from their belief in the resurrection. In our highly secularized world, a world estranged from God, consecrated people continue to bear witness to the fact that God has everything to do with this world. They proclaim God's message of love through what they say and do, and through their willingness to serve in general.

Religious believe that the charism that we were blessed with is ultimately a gift to the church.

A service to the poor

Given the reflection in the previous paragraph and given the nature of our charisms, we see that the poor should be the first to benefit from our efforts. We are not here for ourselves. God guides us to the places where people need us, the poor and the forgotten, to places from which God has been chased or forgotten. That is true for all types of religious life.

This engagement in the world as a place of prayer or a place of service is essential to consecrated life. We might say that the world and the poor of this world are entitled to the help of consecrated people. Here, too, the world of the gospel is proven to be true. The poor are always among us. Time and again, new forms of poverty arise: material and spiritual poverty.

Someone once asked one of my confreres whether his life in the West still made sense, now that so many tasks in the field of education and nursing have been taken over by the government. Although it is true that we are no longer doing the work of pioneers, at least not in the West, this brother responded by saying, "As long as there are poor people in the world, our life will be meaningful and make sense, and we will continue to fulfill our mission in the world."

Pastoral care of vocations also has to do with making sure that, as a matter of service to the world, people who wish to open up to the world on account of a special relationship with God keep coming. If we respect ourselves as an order or congregation, we will continue to take initiatives in the field of pastoral care of vocations. Not in order to guarantee our continued existence, but because we are serving God, the church and the world.

Knowing that the Lord calls upon those whom God desires, we must not stand in God's way, claiming that we have done all that we could and that we had better die than recruit new blood, discouraging young people from participating in that adventure with God.

Even the unfaithful priest Eli became an instrument in the hands of the Lord. It was he who helped Samuel to understand the Lord's calling: "Speak, Lord, for your servant is listening" (1 Samuel 3:9).

To keep calling in the desert

Pastoral care of vocations is not easy, least of all when we find ourselves in a secularized environment where we are inclined to withdraw.

We can think of many reasons why we should not stay involved – the world is not receptive to God's calling; young people are under the influence of all kinds of imaginary and false values; families no longer encourage their children when they claim to have a religious vocation; there are many other ways to serve one's fellow humans or go abroad; there is so much criticism of celibacy, as though it were the ultimate cause of a frustrated existence.

Indeed, we are calling in the desert. By "desert" we mean the lack of young people who feel called to live a consecrated life these days.

All those facts may discourage us or even make us feel guilty. Did we not do the right thing? Was all that we did and were all those thing to which we were so dedicated meaningless? Some religious allow themselves to be misled by those new groups that arise here and there and eventually decide that they have no future.

Maybe we should take a closer look at those new groups and consider what makes them so attractive. Why do they succeed in encouraging new vocations? These groups or movements do not do anything special; in most cases, the members live rather traditional religious lives. But they do pay a lot of attention to the basics of religious life. For example, studying their prayer life, you will notice that they devote attention to their personal as well as to their common prayer life. While visiting the birthplace of Benedict of Nursia, I heard beautiful singing in a church. Much to my surprise I found that only two young monks and two adolescents were singing vespers. During a conversation that I had with one of the monks afterwards, I learned that they had only recently been refounded on the initiative of the general abbot, and that it had taken them only one year to have two postulants, whereas there had not been any new candidates at the enormous abbey in nearby Montecassino for years.

That short conversation gave rise to a series of questions concerning our prayer life and its possible appeal. Do we not claim all too quickly that we can no longer pray together because our numbers have become too small? Do we still pray sincerely or have our prayers become a habit and merely a part of our daily duties? Do we still pay sincere attention to our domestic liturgy or is that just another task that we have to fulfill? Is our participation in the parish enriching the liturgy or are we among the first to leave the church? Do people still see us as a spiritual community or are we no longer any different from ordinary people in that respect? These and other questions may confront us with a number of weaknesses. It is to be hoped that they will encourage us to see those weaknesses as challenges.

Another thing that is remarkable about those new groups is that they are particularly welcoming about their community life. They really make time for one another and try to live that brotherly or sisterly love wholeheartedly. By consciously wearing the religious habit, they wish to demonstrate their unity. In most cases, you meet them in pairs, sent out to proclaim the gospel. This brings us to the apostolic dimension of their lives. One day, a young fraternity decided to make a pastoral tour of China. The group came to ask me some questions. I had been to China recently in order to launch several projects and to offer assistance. I had travelled to China as a "specialist" more than as a religious, using social concern as a way to introduce the church in China. But the brothers wanted to go dressed in their habits in order to proclaim the Word of God. When they came by several months later to report on their visit, I was surprised to learn that they had been able to gather a group of young people around them and had told them about Jesus, all without speaking a single word of Chinese. They already had plans to return the next year. Was I witnessing something of the enthusiasm of the first Christians, something we had lost? Every year, this fraternity welcomes a number of new candidates, while in so many other congregations there have been no new candidates for years. This should encourage us to think – to reflect on the life we lead, on our way of life as such, and on how we might make our life more attractive and appealing for young people who are still called upon by God today.

God has not changed his way of calling, but the environment in which God's voice resonates has thoroughly changed.

Pastoral care of vocations

For a long time, the pastoral care of vocations was not a priority with many orders and congregations. For example, the Jesuits adhered to the conviction that they had to live their lives in a way that was inspiring for young people. That statement is similar to the remark that I used in the introduction to this chapter.

However, in a recent letter from the Superior General of the Jesuits, P.H. Kolvenbach, we read a rather different opinion:

> The service of stimulating vocations for the Society is eminently important and decisive for the future of the Society and the task which it is called to fulfil in the Church. Vocations are a gift from God, but it is a gift that is related to our efforts to discover and stimulate them. Vocations are stimulated by

our praying, by a clear presentation of our charism and mission, by personal contacts with young people in all fields of our apostolic work, by inviting people who are interested to take part in the activities of the Society, by publicising our mission and our saints by means of posters, books, videotapes, and via radio, television and the internet. But those means will not be enough. In order to feel called upon to join the Society in order to give shape to one's personal and Christian life, a personal relationship is indispensable.[58]

We can learn something from Kolvenbach's words. They underline the importance of openness, since communities must welcome young people. Moreover, they stress the importance of a personal witness, of the use of modern means of communication, such as the Internet. We could ask ourselves whether we dare invite young people to participate in our apostolate and whether we are still present among the young and have personal contacts with them.

Those very same questions were raised during the 1997 European Congress on Vocations. The book containing the abstracts from this congress offers interesting thoughts on pastoral care for vocations that we can put into practice now.[59] The book outlines a number of pedagogical principles by which our pastoral care of vocations should be organized. These principles are based on the parable of the sower (Matthew 13:3-8). This parable teaches us something about the first step to be taken: one has to sow. God is the sower, with the help of humans. It is up to us to sow the good seeds. But we are familiar with the parable's talk about thorns, rocky soil, roads on which the seeds are trampled and crushed. Only in good soil do seeds get a chance to germinate. But that does not mean that we will see the results immediately. We need to water, to weed, sometimes to protect them against the sun or against the birds who would otherwise eat them. Those images are all useful ones in the context of our pastoral care of vocations. We need to sow, too, but it is good to know where there is fertile soil today. The season is important, too; young people are sometimes more sensitive to a particular message during a particular period in their life.

The seed of a vocation might well be the smallest of seeds. Maybe it is like the mustard seed, which, once it has started growing, turns into a large tree. Pastoral care of vocations starts with sowing, but God expects a certain degree of competence from us so that the seeds will not be spilled. We must organize, structure and use modern techniques so that the seeds can germinate in fertile soil. However, the sowing is not followed immediately by the harvest. A lot of work must be done before a farmer can take a sickle or combine to get the crops in. Still, according to the aforementioned congress, the various phases involve offering guidance, educating, training and making distinctions. This process corresponds with Jesus' pedagogy, the one that is illustrated in the gospel text where he walks towards Emmaus with his disciples.

In a second phase, the sower becomes a guide who sets off with the young and gives them the opportunity to think things through. It is the aspect of journey. The Lord is invisibly present in the guide and lets the Holy Spirit make her way (Luke 24:13-16). She is there in order to point to the Lord simply by being present. In that phase, the image of the Samaritan woman by the well is often used (John 4:7). What are the wells that young people visit these days? Can we be present there as guides? It is a plea for a focused policy of presence wherever young people gather together. Or maybe we can dig wells ourselves, creating places where young people come because they can discover cores of sincerity there.

It is certain that the guide, in this phase, should approach the young, be present at their sides, try to understand them, and share their faith with them: in other words, draw water from the well with them.

The third phase is all about education, for the story continues, just as with the disciples of Emmaus (Luke 24:17-29).

It boils down to daring to react to suggestions like "I would like to, but ..." or "We were hoping, but ...." That is educating at the heart of the mystery; it is getting to know the young person's story through the scriptures and through the young person's prayers. In that respect, it is important to become Jesus' apprentice and to make his methods our own. He asks questions; he makes references but does not preach. He leaves it to others to discover what it is all about and makes sure that the young get to know Jesus, not as some kind of spiritual or ethical concept, but as a living person who is worth the sacrifice of one's life.

The next two phases, namely the formation/training (Luke 24:30-32) and the making of distinctions (Luke 24:33-35) are not specific elements of our pastoral care of vocations but serve as the framework for the actual formation of the person who feels called by God. In those biblical texts we read how Jesus instructs his disciples on how to become true disciples so that they eventually cry out, "Were not our hearts burning within us ...?" (Luke 24:32). And then, totally changed, they were ready to live up to their commitments. Without delay, they left for Jerusalem in order to proclaim the Good News there as well.

The congress on vocations was preceded by a survey in Europe from which interesting conclusions were drawn.[60] One of the most important of these was that pastoral care of vocations should be situated in a christological and ecclesiological context. We can distinguish four steps:

1) Faith amounts to more than purely spiritual and ethical considerations. It is about Jesus, who is responsible for our deliverance. We must convince young people that it is Christ who is worth the sacrifice of our lives.

2) If young people could get to know Christ in that way, they would feel attracted to the idea of following him. It is about realizing that Jesus calls everyone to follow him. Faith in Jesus is not an informal matter.

3) Then follows the discovery that one does not stand alone, that there is a people of God who follow the path of Christ together, but each with their own charism.

4) Finally, every specific vocation, once it has become clear, has to be situated in the context of the universal vocation to sanctify all the faithful. An integration movement follows the movement of separation.

Among other things in that document, we find a description of how this guidance can be organized. To that purpose four words are used: announce, propose, discern and accompany. Those are the four steps to take in our pastoral care of vocations, and in that order.

In addition, the document contains references to the fairly negative attitude and climate, even in families, when a son or daughter announces that he or she feels called to religious life. Still, we must continue to advance towards the core, and continue to pray for vocations and encourage young people to pray for their own vocation.

Those two interesting documents do not provide complete answers to all the questions concerning pastoral care of vocations, but they allow us to grasp the meaning of the phrase *in verbo tuo*, or "on your word," from the story about the miraculous catch (Luke 5:1-11). Are we not all like those fishermen who came to the disappointing conclusion that they had not caught a single fish by the end of a night of hard work? And then Jesus asked them to "put out into the deep water and let down your nets for a catch" (Luke 5:4). What did Jesus know about fishing that those experienced fishermen did not know? They let down their nets again, but on the other side of the boat this time, on his word, and we all know the result. Their nets could not hold all the fish they caught! We should cherish what Jesus told the apostles afterwards: he promised that they would become fishers of men, inviting them to witness to the Good News, inviting people to come and see, to be bearers of hope.

What are we waiting for to let down our nets on his word?

11

The Future

Many orders and congregations show their openness to sharing their charism with lay people. Formerly, we spoke of passing on the charism; today, we realize that this term was something of a misnomer, as if people are receiving something second-hand. Instead, an understanding developed that we can live the same spirituality by sharing the charism with others. A charism as a gift of the Holy Spirit remains active today so that it can attract people other than religious, and engage them in a new and specific spirituality. Also, new forms of involvement with an order or congregation can originate from within it: co-workers in the apostolate will be strongly inspired by the charism; inspired volunteers will help realize the apostolic mission; lay people will draw their inspiration from the charism to live their Christian faith more intensely; others will join an order or congregation by becoming associate members; youth may engage themselves as effective members on a temporary basis. These are all relatively new forms that partly reshape religious life.

Recent church documents have drawn the attention to these new forms. Three paragraphs of *Vita Consecrata* are devoted to co-operation with lay people (54), to its consequences for the apostolate (55), and to lay volunteers and associate members (56). The 1997 Conference of Major Superiors of Men and the Leadership Conference of Women Religious, the two conferences of major superiors in the United States, held an inquiry about the development of associate membership of the religious life. The Unione Superiori Generali (USG), or the Union of General Superiors in Rome, met for a general meeting in November 1999 about the topic "Sharing in the charisms and spirituality: Consecrated life open to lay people."[61]

These studies and documents gave rise to a new and refreshing vision on the different kinds of associations, requiring us to examine the question of whether associate members are inheritors or truly new members. Is there new growth within consecrated life, or is it an extension of a long tradition? The phenomenon is worth considering when we realize that in 1998 there were 15,000 associate members of women religious congregations in the United States alone.

An extension of a rich past

Fairly soon after monasticism began in the West, it became customary for parents to present their children to abbeys to be educated in Christian virtues. The rules of both Basil and Benedict provide regulations for the formation of these "oblates." Adults could also enter abbeys as converts and start living under the auspices of the abbey after a limited formation of six months' duration. These converts or lay brothers have been part of the abbeys until very recently. It is only since Vatican II that the distinction between lay brother and choir monk was phased out. At the beginning of the mendicant orders in the Middle Ages, there were also new positions for lay people within the abbeys. Along with his actual order of friars, Francis of Assisi founded a secular Third Order to which he gave his own rule in 1221. Thus, from the very beginning of their existence, a secular branch existed within the Franciscans; this was also the case with the Dominicans, the Servites, the Carmelites and the Norbertines. Third Order members strove towards Christian perfection in the world according to the specific spirituality of the order to which they belonged. The church accepted these forms, and many popes took a positive attitude towards this spiritual lifestyle for lay people.

Some Third Orders gave rise to new religious families that were recognized as congregations at a later stage; others became secular institutions.

In the 18th and 19th centuries, many new congregations were founded, and they, too, offered possibilities for lay people. A typical example is Don Bosco's congregation of priests, to which lay people were admitted and given their own formal position in his Salesian society.

If the 1917 Canon Law was rather vague about the founding of lay associations, the new Canon of 1983 says that all religious institutes have the right to found associations of the faithful who share their spirituality and apostolic life (canon 303).

Thus the phenomenon of associate members is not new, but is subject to change over time. When we consider them today we need to see them in the light of Vatican II's new image of church.

A new image of church

The dogmatic constitution on the church, *Lumen Gentium*, introduced a new image of church. Until then, the church had been seen as hierarchical, with lay people playing a minor role; in *Lumen Gentium*, the church was presented as the pilgrim People of God. The understanding of the church as a community became pivotal in the Vatican II documents. Lay people, priests and religious together build *communio* (community) with Christ.

The respective states of life are clearly described in *Lumen Gentium*. Here is what the document says about the lay people:

> But the laity, by their very vocation, seek the kingdom of God by engaging in temporal affairs and by ordering them according to the plan of God. They live in the world, that is, in each and in all of the

secular professions and occupations. They live in the ordinary circumstances of family and social life, from which the very web of their existence is woven. They are called there by God that by exercising their proper function and led by the spirit of the Gospel they may work for the sanctification of the world from within as a leaven. (*LG*, 31)

Christifidelis Laici, the document of the 1987 Synod on Christian Lay People, about the vocation and mission of lay people in the church and in the world, discusses how the various states of life can co-exist. Number 55 of this document says that the states of life are so linked to one another that they are bound together.

Lay people, priests and religious are all expected to live the universal call to holiness in perfect love. However, they differ in the manner in which this call is lived and in their complementarity to one another.

It is the layperson's task to take care of temporal matters and to sanctify them so that their significance for God's plan of salvation is made clear to priests and religious. By living their vocation fully, lay people remind priests and religious that God's presence is realized in everyday life. God is indeed an immanent God who takes on our nature and sets up his tent among humans. Lay people have heard the message of the angel not to remain gazing at heaven; they must make real Jesus' presence in the concrete circumstances of life (Acts 1:11).

Priests are called to make Christ, the Redeemer, present sacramentally. They help religious and lay people approach the transcendent God sacramentally, to make God present in time. There are moments in life when God's presence is specially needed, as well as places where God's sacramental presence is seminal for life.

Finally, religious want to witness to the eschatological character of the church. They testify by their lifestyle that the world is not an end in itself but is directed towards the hereafter. The essence of life according to the religious vows is that consecrated people do not attach a high priority to earthly values but subordinate them to the highest good – the kingdom where God fills their life totally and exclusively. The rest is integrated with this attitude and receives its shape and form from this all-surpassing reality. By their conscious ways of living this reality, consecrated people remind lay people and priests not to lose sight of the ultimate purpose of life on earth. We do not have a lasting dwelling place here on earth; our final dwelling place is in heaven.

Lay people, priest and religious are, therefore, complementary pilgrims who prepare the coming of the kingdom in this world. *Christifideles Laici* refers to two sacred writers, Ambrose and Francis of Sales (*CL*, 55, 56). Both were ahead of their time. Ambrose compares the church to a field where many crops sprout and flowers bloom. He calls the priesthood, virginity and matrimony a rich harvest. In his *Introduction to the Devout Life*, Francis of Sales takes a clear stand on the general vocation to holiness for all people:

> It is an error, or rather a heresy, to try to banish the devout life from the regiment of soldiers, the shop of the mechanic, the court of princes, or the home of married folk. It is true, Philothea, that a purely contemplative, monastic and religious devotion cannot be exercised in such ways of life. But besides these three kinds of devotion, there are several others adapted to bring to perfection those who live in the secular state. Therefore we can and must strive after the life of perfection in whatever circumstances of life. (*CL*, 56)[62]

Charism as meeting place

Our working definition becomes the following: lay people, priests and religious as the People of God are on a journey, drawing from the same sources and being called to universal holiness. I realize that I add a new element to that definition – the source from which all the faithful draw their inspiration, the gospel as the living Word of God. All are called to find their inspiration to live the gospel values in their own place and time, giving rise to something unique and complementary. While all believers draw from the same source, its richness is so great that all believers have more than enough to fill their lives. Charisms can be seen as deeply stirring invitations from the gospel that the Holy Spirit offers as gifts to the faithful. A charism bears fruit when the mysterious combination between the Spirit's gift and the natural talent of the person is realized. Thus it is no longer clear where the natural talent ends and the gift of the Holy Spirit comes in. There is a multiplicity of gifts of the Holy Spirit, of charisms; so we say with the Apostle Paul,

> To each is given the manifestation of the Spirit for the common good. To one is given through the Spirit the utterance of wisdom, and to another the utterance of knowledge according to the same Spirit, to another faith by the same Spirit, to another gifts of healing by the one Spirit, to another the working of miracles, to another prophecy, to another the discernment of spirits, to another various kinds of tongues, to another the interpretation of tongues.
> (1 Corinthians 12:7-10)

Religious congregations return to their founding charism – the one that emerged in their founder or foundress and evolved from an individual gift to a congregational charism. When the pioneers and later members formed the congregation, they shared in the charism so that it became the living source of inspiration down through the generations. A charism is a gift to an individual, but it can also be received by others and by many new generations after that person.

Some communities of religious believed that their charism was given to their consecrated members only. They considered themselves the direct inheritors of the founder's or foundress's charism. But who are we to put limitations on the workings of the Holy Spirit and to lock her up in a cage of human reasoning? The Holy Spirit cannot be restrained but shows her infinite power by a continuous renewal of the church at the most unexpected times and places. Our position, therefore, should be that the charism of a religious institution belongs to the whole church. It is a charism given to a specific person, whose followers give it expression and who consecrate themselves to God in the religious state. But this charism may become a source of inspiration to other people who do not want to live as religious in the first place, but who are inspired by it and find their vocation to holiness in the world.

A charism given to a certain religious institution at a certain moment remains open to others to share it. It is never an exclusive possession of a group; the group cannot monopolize it. Thus, a religious institution represents only one of the possible ways in which a charism can be lived and can bear fruit. Other ways are possible, as some founders realized from the very start of their congregations. As we have seen, Francis of Assisi founded a secular order; Don Bosco offered his charism to priests, religious and lay people from the very start of his congregation.

It is in the line of this new interpretation that we are to read numbers 54 and 56 of the *Vita Consecrata*. The working document of the Synod on Religious Life dealt with the topic when it examined the reciprocal openness of the respective states of life. Number 54 is quite explicit when it says: "In recent years, one of the fruits of the teaching on the Church as communion has been the growing awareness that her members can and must unite their efforts, with a view to cooperation and exchange of gifts, in order to participate more effectively in the Church's mission. This helps to give a clearer and more complete picture of the Church herself, while rendering more effective the response to the great challenges of our time, thanks to the combined contributions of the various gifts." The new image of the church is stressed here again. The central point of co-operation between religious and lay people is situated precisely in the charism: "Today, often as a result of new situations, many Institutes have come to the conclusion that *their charism can be shared with the laity*" (*VC*, 54). This wording is perhaps too weak in view of what we have just said about the development of the charism. Lay people are not invited just to share the charism as a remote member of the family, but are called to live it personally, as a direct inheritor, and to integrate it in their own lives. They are participating in the charism one hundred per cent.

The document emphasizes the dynamics resulting from the renewed co-operation between lay people and religious: "The participation of the laity often brings unexpected and rich insights into certain aspects of the charism, leading to a more spiritual interpretation of it and helping to draw from it directions for new activities in the apostolate" (*VC*, 55). Experiences in some apostolic congregations that shared their charism with lay co-workers point in that direction so that renewal happens to both the spirituality and the apostolic activities. Congregations that have tried to formulate their mission in co-operation with their lay members experienced how their charism was given a boost and became refreshingly active and inspiring to both religious and lay people.

Religious institutions can go a step further and admit lay people to their ranks. In number 56 of *Vita Consecrata* we find various forms: associate members, volunteers in the apostolate and temporary associates. On the other hand, consecrated people may join new church groups in order to enrich their own charism. All in all, a plea is made to arrive at a clearly defined structure so that the respective groups within an institution know and live their specificity and complementarity.

The inquiry set up by religious women in the United States gives lay people their own niche when they join with a religious institution.[63] The volunteers, mainly young people, work temporarily in the apostolate and are given special training for it and a formal statute. Besides them, there are lay missionaries who are sent to a developing country for a set period of time. Finally, there are the associate members whose main characteristic is that they fully participate in the charism of the institution and live it by means of spiritual exercise, by co-operating in the apostolate and even taking part in the community life.

The report of the general meeting of the USG goes into detail concerning the full participation of associate members and its advantages to both religious and lay people.

The rise of the associate members opens the dossier of the founding members. When a religious institution decides to accept associate members, a new institution is founded. If the charism had started a religious community, it is now at the basis of a new association of lay people. It expands the religious institution, which must be rethought. It becomes an institution where both religious and associate members are at home, and this fact needs to be seen structurally. When associates are recognized by the church, they will be given a position in the organization of the religious institution, its chapters and government. It is important for the religious themselves to be involved in order to form church genuinely with the associate members.

Charisms, which were concretized by religious communities, can bring their prophetic voice to lay people's search for a renewed evangelical Christian life. The vocation and mission of lay people can have a new application, with the understanding that these lay people should not consider themselves semi-religious but retain their secular character. In fact, they should become better lay people by sharing in the charism, and start living their vocation and mission as lay people in the church in a more intense way. At the same time, it may give rise to a greater input and stronger position of the lay person in the church that can help to get rid of the clerical mentality. It would be wrong if lay people lost their secular character by associating with a religious institution. Therefore it is important that admitting lay people is to be done carefully, without blurring the specificity of either the religious or the lay people.

What still needs to be clarified is the great influence that parents can have on the education of their own children. Not only the co-operation in the apostolate, but also their family life can be deepened by it.

Finally, we should also consider what initiatives could be taken by the associate members. That is why it is necessary for the group of associates to have their own representatives who consult with and act under the responsibility of the superiors of the religious institution.

Some new questions

When a religious institution, usually after due consideration and guided by the Holy Spirit, decides to admit associate members, a lot of questions must be asked. A specific training program needs to be created and a number of religious, in consultation with their superior, must be responsible for the training. At the same time, room must be made for the dynamics of the new group as the concrete working of the Holy Spirit. The emerging spirituality within the group of associate members will not be just a carbon copy of the spirituality of the religious. Although both groups draw from the same source, the result will be different because the vocation and mission of lay people differ from the religious in their life circumstances.

Much attention must be paid to the mentoring of the religious themselves because the integration of a new group within the congregation is not clear and is going to change its image. Both religious and associate members must try to understand, respect, encourage and support one another; after all, they are to form one group, one congregation. This approach presupposes that they get to know one another, meet, speak, pray and listen together. The respective communities will have to see how they can welcome and integrate the associate members into the community activities.

A useful exercise for religious and associate members is the exploration of the charism in a common effort to detect principles that form the building blocks of their own spirituality and that open up new areas for the mission of both religious and associate members.

In order to be able to speak about sharing a charism, a number of conditions need to be fulfilled. Since the gift of the Holy Spirit – a charism – is always freely given, it cannot be forced onto someone. Lay people must be receptive of this type of gift. Consequently, it is rather delicate for a religious community to start to increase the formation of associate members.

However, congregations need to be ready and willing to share their charism. To not share our charism would imply that we still hold to a pre-conciliar image of church. Without that kind of openness and willingness, it is impossible to share our charism.

Reality has taught us that this may take some time with some members. It is a slow process on which the presence of associate members can exert a positive influence, stimulating a real transformation of individual religious or the whole community.

This sharing of the charism is a process that requires much creativity, but that can be refreshing to the community. The fact that lay people allow themselves to be moved by a charism that was meaningful to the church years ago can restore faith in that charism. To some groups, among which the number of vocations to consecrated life has dropped, the arrival of associate members can give an injection of life and enthusiasm. The vocation to the associate membership cannot replace the vocation to live a consecrated life, but the two are complementary to the extent that their unique characters are preserved and strengthened.

Finally, the religious institution must adapt its organizational structure so that the associate members are not only spiritually but also structurally integrated.

Does this mean that a new wind is blowing through the life of religious communities? That a shoot may grow into a tree among the familiar trees? We know that no human power can withstand God's power if it is the work of the Holy Spirit. Religious and religious institutions are invited to listen to the rustling of God's Spirit.

Notes

1 A Spirituality

1   Joan Chittister, *The Fire in These Ashes: A Spirituality of Contemporary Religious Life* (Kansas City: Sheed & Ward, 1995), 184.

2   Statistics of the Association of Major Superiors in Belgium and the Union of Religious in Belgium.

3   J. B. Metz, *Religieuzen naar een nieuwe tijd? Mystiek en politiek van de navolging* (Boxtel: Katholieke Bijbelstichting, 1977), 88.

4   Timothy Radcliffe, "De beer en de monnik," in *Unie*, september 1999, no. 4, 3.

5   Cornelius Ernst, *The Theology of Grace* (Dublin: Mercier, 1974), 72.

2 A Way of Life

6   Brothers of Charity, *Rule of Life: Moved by Charity*, Ghent, 1986, no. 2.

7   Murray Stein, *Jung's Map of the Soul* (Chicago: Open Court, 2001), 43–44.

8   Koen De Meester, *Laurent, In de Zon van Gods aanwezigheid* (Oudenaerde: Carmelitans, 1994), 50.

9   Anselm Grün, *Heaven Begins with You: Wisdom from the Desert Fathers* (New York: Crossroad, 1999).

3 A New Challenge

10   *Vita Consecrata* (Post-synodal Apostolic Exhortation on Consecrated Life), 1996.

11   Joan Chittister, *The Fire in These Ashes*, 47.

12   Thomas Aquinas, in Seán Sammon, *Religious Life in America* (New York: St. Paul's, 2002), 204.

13   J. B. Metz and T. R. Peters, *Passie voor God* (Hertogenbosch: Katholieke Bijbelstichting, 1992), 19–26.

14 Joan Chittister, *The Fire in These Ashes*, 11.

15 Enzo Bianchi, *Si tu savais le don de Dieu : La vie religieuse dans l'Église* (Bruxelles: Lessius, 2001), 285.

16 Ibid., 285.

17 St. Teresa of Jesus, Poesías 30, in *The Collected Works of St. Teresa of Avila*, vol. III, tr. K. Kavanaugh, OCD, and O. Rodriguez, OCD (Washington DC: Institute of Carmelite Studies, 1985), 386 no. 9, tr. by John Wall.

18 André Dodin, *Vincent de Paul and Charity* (New Rochelle, NY: New City Press, 1993), 126.

4 A Framework

19 Joan Chittister, *The Fire in These Ashes*, 47.

20 J. B. Metz and T.R. Peters, *Passie voor God*, 19–26.

21 J. B. Metz, *Religieuzen naar een nieuwe tijd*, 32.

22 Joan Chittister, *The Fire in These Ashes*, 53.

23 Augustine, *The Confessions* (Nairobi: Paulines, 2003), 192.

5 Making Room in Our Hearts

24 Joseph Bernardin, *The Gift of Peace* (London: Darton, Longman and Todd, 1998), 120.

25 Mother Teresa, *Liefde kent geen grenzen* (Tielt: Lannoo, 1976), 104.

26 Etty Hillesum, *Het verstoorde leven* (Haarlem, De Haan, 1982), 197.

27 Francis Xavier Nguyên Vân Thuân, *Testimony of Hope* (Boston: Pauline Books and Media, 2000), 222.

28 Abraham Joshua Heschel, *In het licht van zijn aanschijn* (Utrecht: Bijleveld, 2000), 160.

29 Enzo Bianchi, *Si tu savais le don de Dieu*, 285.

6 United in God

30 A.A.A. Terruwe, *De liefde bouwt een woning* (Lochem : De Tijdstroom, 1983), 106.

31 Brother Christian's Testament: http://www.ocso.org/HTM/testc-vv.htm (accessed June 7, 2007).

7 Religious Leadership

32 Godfried Kard. Danneels, "Christelijk geïnspireerd leiderschap" (unpublished text, 1984), 20.

33 *The Holy Rule of St. Benedict* (translated by Rev. Boniface Verheyen, osb), 1949.

34 Wil Deckse, *Een levensregel voor beginners, Benedictijnse spiritualiteit voor het dagelijkse leven* (Tielt: Lannoo, 2000), 126.

35 *The Holy Rule of St. Benedict*, no. 2, 33.

36 Anselm Grün, *Menschen Führen, Leben wecken* (Münsterschwarzach, 1998), 20.

37 Robert K. Greenleaf, *The Servant-leader Within a Transformative Path* (New York: Paulist Press, 2003), 32.

38 Ibid., 51.

39 Ibid., 52.

40 Ibid., 19.

41 Ibid.

8 Moved by Charity

42 J. B. Metz, *Religieuzen naar een nieuwe tijd?*, 43–67.

43 Ibid., 29.

44 Joan Chittister, *The Fire in These Ashes*, 23.

45 J. B. Metz, *Religieuzen naar een nieuwe tijd?*, 56.

46 Ibid., 60.

47 Ibid., 45.

48 Joan Chittister, *The Fire in These Ashes*, 11.

49 Jan Koenot, *Religieus leven nu en morgen* (Brussel: V.H.O.B.-U.R.B., 1999), 19.

9 Growing Older

50 John Paul II, Apostolic Exhortation *Familiaris Consortio*, 1981, 27.

51 *Insegnamenti di Giovanni Paolo II*, V, 3 (1982), 125.

52 Leo Missinne, *Leven toevoegen aan de jaren* (Leuven: Davidsfonds, 1996), 151.

53 Teilhard de Chardin in Leo Missine, *Leven toevoegen aan de jaren*, 75.

54 Pope John Paul II, *Over bejaarden: Toespraken* (Amersfoort: De Horstink, 1989), 92.

55 Rainer Maria Rilke, *Letters to a Young Poet*, www.pa56.org/ross/rilke.htm (accessed May 2, 2007).

10 Vocations

56 Tertullian, *Apology*, Chapter XXXIX.

57 Canon P. J. Triest in a homily, 1802.

58 P. H. Kolvenbach, November 1997. Letter to the Institute.

59 *De nouvelles vocations pour une nouvelle Europe* (document final du Congrès Européen sur les vocations au sacerdoce et à la vie consacrée en Europe), 1997, 116.

60 *La pastorale des vocations dans les Églises particulières d'Europe: document préparatoire* (Œuvre pontificale pour les vocations ecclésiastiques), 1997, 77.

11 The Future

61 U.S.G., Charisme et Spiritualité, 56ᵉ Conventus Semestralis, novembre 1999, Rome, 105.

62 Francis de Sales, *Introduction à la vie dévote*, I, III: Œuvres complètes, Monastère de la Visitation, Annency 1893, III, 19–21.

63 Dawn Gibeau, "Lay associates flock to religious orders," *National Catholic Reporter*, Feb. 16, 1996), 13–14.